Desiring
Paradise

... a true story of succumbing to the dream

Karin W. Schlesinger

Printed in the United States of America
ISBN # 0-9673721-2-7

Cover Design by: SkyMax Design, Concord, NH
Typesetting and copyediting by: SkyMax Design, Concord, NH

Conch Publications
P.O. Box 1559
St. John, United States Virgin Islands, 00831

e-mail: kaybob@islands.vi

To Bob, with whom life is always an adventure.
And to our wonderful friends, without whom our
adventures would be less fun . . .

all dreams are possible.

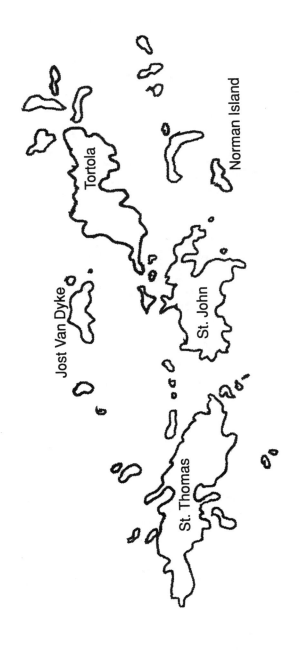

Norman Island

Tortola

Jost Van Dyke

St. John

St. Thomas

Acknowledgments

As with any book, this one would not be a reality if it were not for many special people: Jan, Mary, Joe, Gerry, Janine, Marcie, Bob, Mike, Jessie, Jay, Andre, Karen, John, Pat, Dan, Maureen, Barbara, Michelle, Marianne, Dorothy, Shelly, Charlie, Chris, Diane, Will, Liz, Pamela, Tim, Elanore, Ron, Marsha, David, Chuck, Katie, George, Issaih, Laura, Moe, Aaron, Shelia, Cindy, Jim, Suzanne, Rob, Beverly, Joe, Ted, Ed and Frank - you all made a difference.

Book production and publication thanks go to:
Book-mart Press, Inc. for pre-press and printing
and SkyMax Design for the beautiful cover,
typesetting and copyediting.

A special thanks to Birdie who helped me keep
the dream alive and kept me sane through it all.

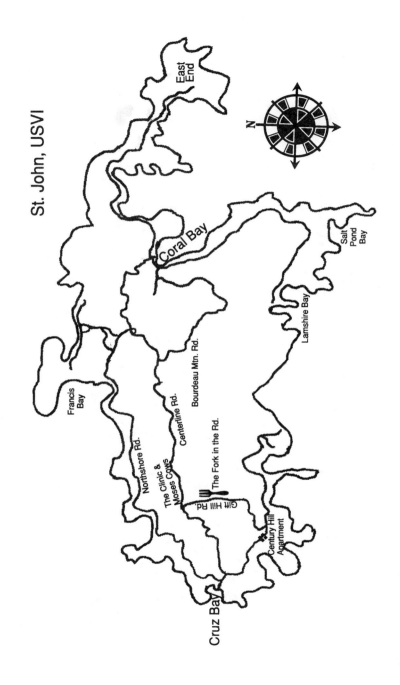

St. John, USVI

East End

N

Coral Bay

Salt Pond Bay

Lamshire Bay

Francis Bay

Northshore Rd.

The Clinic &
Moses Cows

Centerline Rd.

Bourdeau Mtn. Rd.

The Fork in the Rd.

Gift Hill Rd.

Century Hill
Apartment

Cruz Bay

Chapter One
Island Fantasy

We stayed at the Maho Bay Campground at Little Maho Bay on our first visit to St. John, which may have had something to do with it. Perhaps we swallowed some rare organism in the water or breathed in some pollen from a rare but undiscovered island flower that grew nearby. Our island friends insist we must have.

It's a documented fact that in the first half of this century, Ms. Ethel W. McCully (1886-1990) was passing by this same area on a Tortola bound sloop when suddenly enthralled, she jumped ship and waded ashore at little Maho. Ms. McCully was already well past her prime with white hair but a strong disposition when she arrived with the desire to live out her years here on St. John. She soon bought the land above, built a house, became an island legend and stayed for the rest of her long life.

Little Maho Bay seemed to have this same effect on many that glimpsed it for the first time. For at least fifteen St. Johnians we know personally, just one trip to Maho made them go native. But this is our story:

It's true that Bob and I became enamored during our first stay at Maho Bay. But it was the huge plywood sign in the shape of a salad fork elsewhere on the island that first intrigued us. There were no words on the sign, nor any restaurant nearby, just a narrow dirt road ambling away from the main road we'd driven down to explore. Bob was the first to understand we'd arrived at a fork in the road as he gamely steered our rental vehicle onto the dusty side path in search of adventure.

That evening, I sat with my husband on the balcony at Pusser's in tiny Cruz Bay, weary but exhilarated from our island explorations. As we watched the sun setting over St. Thomas past the palm tree lined beach below, Bob and I sighed in unison that we could live here forever. Probably everyone who has viewed the sunsets from Pusser's balcony has had the same thoughts, but for us it marked the beginning of our dream.

On each subsequent vacation to St. John the dream beckoned - at the beach, on the deck of a rented house, or driving slowly past goats blocking the roadway. Our vacations were each held to a higher standard of living than the one before. Campground visits evolved into house rentals, each one more extravagant than the last. And with each vacation, we fell more in love with our future home. And yes, like Ethel McCully, we swam at Maho Bay often. But we also giggled as we traveled past the plywood fork.

Our future was finally decided by rakes - not forks. It was a typical cool fall day at our modest New England home and our yard was knee deep in oak leaves. Resting on our patio swing in mid-afternoon, Bob and I reminisced how far we'd come since we'd met. With twenty-three bags of raked leaves ready for the garbage man and more still to rake, our future looked dismal and boring.

Bob and I were both exhausted and ready for a change in life-style. Some good friends of ours had recently pulled up their middle-class stakes and moved to Juneau, Alaska to start a new life. Bob was jealous. With winter just around the corner, I thought they were crazy. Still, these folks were actually living an adventure - and they seemed so happy. It was inspiring to consider a new life.

Our exhaustion put us in the mood to dream. I brought out pens and paper and suggested that we each rank the top ten spots in the world where we'd like to live. We shared the results slowly. As we worked our way up from 10th place, it was apparent that Bob and I were a world apart. For me it was the Beaujolais region of France. For him, the wilds of Nepal made sense. The chuckling and incessant giggling at each other's concepts of Paradise slowed us down. Bob's Mount Everest suggestion begged me to query "so you'll be moving there with your next wife?" while the thought of moving to a desert brought tears of laughter to the eyes of my whitewater kayaking husband. By the time we got to the top of our lists, I was resigned to living in our little cape-styled New England home forever.

Then my husband announced his number one concept of Paradise.

"St. John in the US Virgin Islands."

I was struck silent. Most of my list was just a joke, but not this one. Bob's face had become devoid of all expression. St. John had no snow-covered mountains or water for kayaking or even drinking, but he was serious. I shuttered my eyes as I revealed my number one selection.

"St. John, USVI." Only silence followed.

As I lifted my eyes to see his reaction, I saw the corners of Bob's mouth start to turn upward until they broke into widest grin I had ever seen! I didn't know at the time, but I'm told my own smile was huge. We grabbed our rakes, faced each other, and extending the tines we gave each other a momentous "high five". Our world had changed forever.

Excitedly, we discussed specifics. It seemed natural that we should 'just do it' but being close to middle aged we had the baggage of our lives to consider. Bob and I sat there on the swing talking for hours, even as darkness and cold descended around us. Everything about a move to St. John seemed right. It would be Paradise. We envisioned ourselves with weekends at the beach, with no leaves to rake or snow to shovel and the endless possibilities of starting a new life from scratch. Ten years from now - we were not risk-takers.

Bob and I had worked hard to own our home, had friends and family nearby, and were somewhat happily employed at the time. Starting over completely was a scary proposition, but how could we earn a living on a remote island? For those who can carry their life possessions in a backpack and take each day as it comes, a move to Paradise might be simple. But we had complexities in our life and deep Yankee roots. We were enchanted with our Paradise, but were we committed to such a dramatic change to our life-style?

I shared our plan with my best friends while Bob, in his typical quiet fashion, said nothing outside the home. My friends first thought I was kidding, and then challenged the seriousness of our plans, in that way only close friends dare.

"What happens if you change your mind, Karin?" they asked.

"It doesn't matter," I said, although my heart began to beat faster. "That won't happen."

"What happens if Bob changes his mind?" they asked.

"He won't," I said with more confidence than I felt.

They weren't convinced and their concerns admittedly struck close to home. I'd been married once before. My ex-husband was a wonderful man who'd relocated for the sake of a career move I felt I had to take. He had been miserable in his newly adopted home and I took too long to notice. We drifted apart, wanting different things in life. Still, I was confident that I'd learned from the past. Moving to St. John someday was something Bob and I both wanted.

With our fantasy defined, Bob and I began to develop a framework for the ten-year plan that would change many times before we moved. We daydreamed out loud almost daily about how we might earn a living on St. John. Starting a business seemed the most logical route. Our ideas ranged from selling holographic keepsakes of the islands, to helping people develop Internet web pages, to running a kayak guide service. Most businesses go under quickly due to a lack of capital and it would take years to save enough money to launch any business successfully. I couldn't really picture either of us being happy just selling palm frond hats to tourists on a beach. There had to be a more concrete way to make a living.

Like many folks, we had very little cash at our disposal. Admittedly, we had minimal debt - cars, home, and an occasional large purchase, but nothing else. Seldom had we considered budgeting, but we did live within our means. There was no credit card debt - we'd worked on eliminating that for years. We bought what we wanted when we wanted it - there were always new 'toys' and 'gadgets' - but in truth, our needs were simple.

Unlike many married couples, Bob and I never fought over money. We kept two separate checking and savings accounts and each wrote a check for half of every bill that came in. It worked. Bob paid for the stamps, mailed the checks and snookered me on the phone bill every month. But we were content. To escalate our savings and begin tracking our expenses, it would make things simpler to first combine our accounts. Joint savings and checking accounts. What a concept. After seven years of marriage, it was time.

Research had always been important for any major household purchase. Bob and I approached the fantasy of living in Paradise with this in mind. A spiral notebook was designated for writing out our thoughts and ideas on every topic applicable to the move. Every week we'd come up with a new idea for developing a business, but nothing seemed to excite both of us with the same enthusiasm. While we had skills useful in high-tech industries, we had no small business skills or hobbies that we thought could be turned into a viable business on a small island. So we fantasized.

We stopped buying new gadgets we saw advertised. More often than not, our old toys sufficed. This drastically increased our savings from disposable income at a surprising rate. According to our notebook, our joint savings increased fast and I soon wondered if we needed ten years. More likely, the rush of excitement I got each time I looked at a picture from Paradise caused my impatience.

Occasionally Bob dug out mementos from St. John and I bought magazines with articles about the Virgin Islands. My husband was the type of person who saved every piece of paper or receipt he'd ever received. When the weather got bad, or he needed a little lift, Bob pulled out a huge file with every St. John brochure and flyer imaginable and hundreds of photos, culled from previous vacations. Late in the evenings, I got on my computer and searched the Internet for information on any subject that could help our plans. These activities kept warm Caribbean thoughts prevalent in our household throughout the cold New England winter.

Years ago I'd brought back a unique souvenir from St. John, which was buried somewhere in our basement. It was an old USVI license plate that had been recycled and hand painted by some local trying to make a few tourist dollars. I rediscovered it in a large box of junk long forgotten and got Bob to attach the plate to the front of my car, as a vanity plate proclaiming to the world our pipe dream. It was noticed and commented on wherever I drove. The most peculiar one came from a traffic cop encountered on a visit to Bob's mom in up-state New York. As the policeman motioned our car to the side of the road, Bob tried to read his mind.

"He's going to give you a ticket for that license plate, I'll bet. Expired official license plates are illegal as vanity plates, but you wouldn't listen to me." I was sure Bob was right and prepared for the worst as the police-man moseyed across the intersection with a smile on his face.

"Did you drive all the way here from there?" he motioned to my vanity plate. "It must have been a long drive." This guy was serious. Maybe he thought there was an ocean bridge from Florida. Regard-less, he'd just stopped us to voice his awe.

"Uh, yes. It's certainly a long way away. But we love upstate New York," I smiled without rancor. And then cop turned his head to check out another vehicle and we slid away, hoping he wouldn't no-tice the Massachusetts plate on the back of my car.

"Lucky", Bob muttered.

"Yeah - we are," I said smugly. After all, we were moving to Paradise someday.

I felt happier and younger than I had for years. Bob said our singular focus on the future was the reason we were acting like newlyweds all over again. Whatever the reason, our lives had gained a new sense of vigor.

But, a jolt of reality made us reconsider the whole idea. My father became very sick while in Florida at the end of my parents' first cruise ship vacation. Feeling ill, he stopped their rental car in front of a police station then went inside to get directions to a hospital. Apparently he collapsed inside the door and within moments was being routed to a hospital by ambulance. My mom stayed to answer the authorities' questions and was then directed to the hospital where my father was taken. Or so she was told. Five hours and three hospitals later, she found him.

My dad was in intensive care for over six weeks. Mom, who hadn't spent more than a few days apart from my father in forty-nine years, found herself alone in Miami without a local support system. Ironically, Miami Beach was where my parents had fallen in love and married so long ago. But, the area bore little resemblance to that friendly town of long ago. It was confusing at best and in some ways terrifying for someone so unprepared to be suddenly alone and a thousand miles from home. A major boat show was in town, and Mom could only find a room far away from the hospital for the first couple of days.

After the boat show left town, she took up residence in the closest motel to the hospital. It was not a safe neighborhood. My two brothers and I took turns flying down to be with them both, and especially to make sure Mom was safe. Nothing could convince her to move to a nicer location even a few minutes farther away from the hospital. It was a very trying situation for all.

I spent almost every other week that winter in Miami, attempting to keep my job by working when I could with my trusty notebook computer. It was Tele-commuting at its worst. I felt guilty as I worried about how fast I was spending money, since every penny was supposed to be saved for Paradise. And, despite long work hours and regular conference calls with my staff, I was risking my job with an unsympathetic boss. But, family was more important than anything, so Miami came first.

Our moving plans were reconsidered more than once over the realization that if we moved to St. John, our families would be over two thousand miles away. We wouldn't be close by to help with any crisis, and with aging parents it mattered. Yes, Miami was closer geographically speaking to the Virgin Islands than New England. But most likely any future crisis would occur up North.

The incident taught me a lot. I learned new respect for my mother, with her iron disposition and tremendous inner strength. My relationship with my father had always been strong but this crisis strengthened that bond. I got to know my two brothers on a different level and learned to value their individuality. Then, around Easter my father came home and life slowly got back to normal.

Despite the Miami ordeal, once spring arrived in earnest the urge to move became stronger. We shortened the timeframe for the move from ten years to five, nixing the plan to open our own business. Five years was enough time to learn some useful skills and save enough money to live on for at least a year. A first year budget for Paradise was drafted - it was depressing. We were hedging our bets at finding quick jobs, but living for a year without any income was daunting. Five years seemed like a long time away.

We did crazy things to maximize our savings. Purchases were made using only paper money and never with loose change. Every evening, Bob and I sorted the coins we'd accumulated that day. It's amazing with this approach how fast our extra coins added up to significant savings. We saved over three thousand dollars this way. Bob saved our soda and beer cans for recycling and reimbursement. This worked well until we stopped buying soda and found cheaper ways to satisfy our taste buds. With every paycheck we tried to save more than the paycheck before. And we did. Our friends said we had money on the brain and they were right.

Bob and I welcomed every spring season by trekking to Vermont for the first camping trip of the year. For him, the West River kayak weekend was a religious experience. I called this annual trek my "be a good wife weekend". The State owned campground opened pre-season solely to accommodate hundreds of whitewater enthusiasts from all over who were eager to emerge from their winter hibernation. Camping in the cold unpredictable weather and surrounded by slowly melting pockets of ice and snow added to the adventure.

The first evening brought handfuls of people wandering into our campsite, drawn by the roaring campfire, sounds of laughter and the smell of our extravagant Epicurean efforts over open fire. Everyone stalled the inevitable, staying up late and toasting their bodies before facing their cold bedding. The kayakers, including Bob, woke early the next morning. Bundled in their drysuits and helmets, they resembled aliens as they roamed the campground, telling tall tales and lingering over their coffee. This stalling ritual, as usual, lasted late into the morning hours as the kayakers wound up their courage to face the frigid water and prove spring had arrived.

I wasn't around to witness the morning ritual this time. A cold drizzle welcomed me when I tentatively unzipped the tent that morning. If it had been only two degrees colder, it would have been sleet. I quietly called out to the neighboring tent where my good friend Birdie was sleeping. Birdie came every year though she had no interest in kayaking and she hated camping in cold wet weather. It was the all-day adventures we had away from the campground that kept her coming back. We were gone before most kayakers were awake that morning. They thought we were anxious to explore, but it was the thought of the car heater that got us motivated. As our toes warmed, our smiles spread and we headed out for our annual adventure.

Never had Birdie or I allowed a map to dictate our hearts as we whimsically explored the back roads of Vermont. A quilting barn, homemade fudge from a roadside vendor, new roads to explore and lots of laughter made the day pass swiftly. While I tried out ideas for eking out a living in Paradise, my girlfriend teased me that I would never move and give up the West River weekends. That evening we cooked an extravagant candlelit dinner while listening to river tales from kayakers who had never ever ventured beyond the water or the campground running alongside. I kept quiet about reminding Bob about the lack of water and kayaking in Paradise.

The West River weekend hadn't changed our resolve. Bob and I had been visiting bookstores every month to purchase new books on any subject imaginable that would inspire us or help us realize our dreams.

I'd built a small library on early retirement, living simplistically, job searches, home based businesses, and of course, Caribbean living. Each book provided fresh ideas and wisdom we would need. We're both avid readers, but we limited ourselves to the local library to borrow books on subjects we used to buy regularly for pure enjoyment.

By summer, Bob and I were unconsciously shrinking the timeframe again. Whenever we told others of our plans, they inevitably asked when we'd be moving. Our timeframe had been narrowed to five years only a couple of months earlier, but now we often said "three to five years" and sometimes "at least three years out" without thinking.

Our timeframe was far enough in the future so that our friends thought it still a fantasy and didn't take us seriously. Their confidence was not improved by our added caveat: "If we don't move, at least we'll have more money saved than we ever thought possible". This statement was said so often it almost became our mantra.

One spring day the "If" got stuck in my throat. Why could we never bring ourselves to say "When" instead of "If"? Out came the notebook, and into the night I contemplated the numbers and the timeline, determined to pinpoint the elusive "When".

Numbers don't lie. Being the daughter of a successful accountant in a small city, I'd learned that simple truth. Bob and I had both agreed that our retirement money could not be compromised. And our planned move to Paradise included the determination not to move until we'd stashed away enough to be above the poverty line when we retired some twenty-five years away. We needed enough money to live on for a year in case there were no jobs, and money for the move itself. My father's voice sounded in my head over and over that night: "stay conservative and the numbers won't lie". Ignoring pleas to come to bed, I continued working the numbers. I woke Bob up at three in the morning to tell him the amazing news.

"That's nice, dear. Come to bed," was his sleepy response.

Suspecting a conversation was futile, I tried to take his advice. Over my shoulder, I heard a muted "Can't we, Karin? One more vacation first?" but when I turned to respond, I realized my husband was talking in his sleep.

"We'll need to, and soon," I murmured into his ear before I turned away and let sleep come.

We vacationed again on St. John that fall. A full year had passed since we'd begun planning our permanent move and our ten-year plan had turned into a firm three-year plan but we were keeping it a secret. We were already third of the way to Paradise. It was a heady thought. A few days later, our secret was out.

I remember distinctly that moment frozen in time. It was late afternoon at our rental villa in Rendezvous Bay about three-quarters of the way through our stay on the island. The five of us were cooling off in and around our private pool. Bob and I had spent the afternoon with a real estate agent researching for the future. Our relatives, meanwhile, had explored the back roads and beaches of St. John. The house shaded the setting sun and the gentle trade winds were perfect. My brother Joe was making rum punches for everyone with exotic juices he'd bought at an open-air stand in town, while reggae music from a poolside radio gave him rhythm. It was a time for reflecting and philosophizing. In a moment of weakness, I blurted our secret.

"We're definitely moving here in the next two years," I announced, eyeing Bob as he closed his eyes to the shocked faces around him, then floated gently to the center of the pool.

"Really?" Joe had stopped his stirring with a frown. "I thought that was years from now," chimed his wife.

"We won't be living like this - that's for sure," I added quickly.

"Yeah, we'll be too poor." Only my husband's voice hinted he was awake and aware.

"Will it matter?" my sister-in-law asked. To her it would have mattered. Joe and Janine preferred the material world. I knew my heart and could have easily answered, but I didn't. The seconds stretched long against the reggae beat.

"No." floated the answer. "No way" I sighed, though happy Bob had verbalized it first.

"You two are really going to do it?" Bob's sister Dee asked, excited and supportive. While she owned a small but hectic business in Manhattan, Dee had told us earlier in the day that she could see herself waiting tables if she could live in this wonderful place.

'That soon?" Joe asked doubtfully, the drink preparations now forgotten. He thought that our plans were a passing whim that we'd tire of in a few months. To be fair, my childhood was littered with half-finished projects that I'd started with enthusiasm but got bored with when they took too much effort to complete.

"Will you buy a house?" Janine jumped in. Her beautiful New Hampshire home and gardens were also her hobby. Bob, quietly floating towards me, moved nary a muscle and I knew he was waiting for my answer.

"Probably not - I doubt we can afford it," I admitted. Our day had burst that bubble of hope unless we put off our plans to move for many years. I knew it and Bob knew it but we hadn't discussed the outcome. His eyes still closed, my husband instinctively grasped my hand as he announced "It doesn't matter". We both knew that living on St. John would be much different and much more modest than that of a vacation getaway.

"Lots of hurricane damaged places - those may be affordable," Janine persisted, trying to be helpful.

"Not even," said Bob, remembering the extraordinarily priced shacks we'd visited that day.

"Won't you be bored after a while?" Joe asked, as he began passing out the beverages.

"Not a prayer," I said with conviction. Surprisingly I heard my husband add, "I'll miss having a pool though." Before I could react, Dee jumped in. She wanted the dream, if not for herself, then for her brother.

"But you don't have a pool now, except on vacation," she reminded him. A mumbled "True" was his only reply.

"Does it matter?" she asked. I knew the answer before his considered "No", but I also understood that my husband could float forever in this vacation pool and die happy.

"So you're really going to do it." Joe finally accepted reality.

"Within two years!" Dee was already planning her next vacation.

"Yes." I raised my glass. "Yes." My husband raised his.

"Why?" Joe's wife needed to understand.

"Because it feels right," I said while clinking my glass to my darling husband's.

"Yeah," he agreed as he proposed a toast to Paradise.

Island Facts

*St. John is located three miles to the east of St.
Thomas in the USVI. The island consists of 20
square miles of mostly mountainous terrain. Less
than 9 miles across from east to west, it's only
about 4 miles wide from north to south. Almost
2/3 of the island falls under the jurisdiction of
the VI National Park, providing visitors and
residents with plentiful opportunities to com-
mune with nature. The island population is less
than 5,000 people. There is no traffic-light, no
trash pickup service, no high school and no
airport on-island. Ferries run regularly to St.
Thomas, "the Big City" to most St. Johnians
(JOE-nians).*

Chapter Two
Commitment to Paradise

A couple of months before that vacation, Hurricane Marilyn had devastated the islands. Power had been restored to the villa we'd rented only two days prior to our arrival. It was an eye-opening experience. On the surface, much of St. John was back on its feet, but there were very few tourists - less than we'd ever seen before. Many restaurants were closed or offering only limited menus. On St. Thomas, the devastation was visible everywhere.

The Federal Emergency Management Agency was still providing on-site assistance and assessment. Their donated "FEMA Blue" tarps were visible everywhere on St. Thomas, covering or replacing roofs destroyed by the storm. There were few buildings that looked unscathed. Back on St. John, while there were FEMA tarps visible, these blue landmarks were few and far between. Still, we saw a house that had slid right down a mountain with the people inside. Luckily, they survived.

Bob pointed out one home we'd previously admired high on a distant ridge, where now a familiar speck of blue gleamed in the sun. As we drove closer and approached from a different angle, the home seemed unscathed. Rounding the last switchback to the house, the source of the blue became evident. A tarp with "FEMA" written on it had been cut up and turned into awnings on one side of the home. Past another curve, we spied our favorite plywood fork in the road. It even boasted a new coat of paint. All was returning to normal, St. Johnian style, and I was heartened.

One local St. Johnian summed up his opinions on the differences between the islands: "On St. Thomas they wait for the insurance folks to come through and then they'll do repairs, but here on St. John we tend to pitch in and help each other first." As an afterthought he added, "then we pray for the insurance money to make us whole".

Whether it was true or not, this approach to community life on St. John was a comforting thought. It made some sense - St. John is a relatively rural island, unlike the more urban St. Thomas.. The local St. John *Tradewinds* newspaper was filled with stories about people helping people and the quick progress being made to return things to normal and was very upbeat considering the devastation that had occurred two months before.

Consciously during the vacation, Bob and I attempted to uncover the flaws in our Paradise. I saw cockroaches larger than I thought possible. We drank water that locals qualified as 'good', but which we couldn't stand the taste of. Millions of no-see-ums, those little sand fleas that seem to prefer fresh tourists for dinner, dined nightly on my legs. I scraped my knees on the uneven pavements and Bob lost his prescription glasses. Joe got two flat tires in just one day of touring the island in a rental vehicle. We waited for ferries, waited in long lines at businesses and were occasionally treated rudely by the supposedly pleasant locals. I never did find a good cup of coffee.

We met people who were negative about life in general and experienced the frustration of trying to buy a simple spiral notebook anywhere on the island. I turned off the shower while lathering up but ran out of water regardless. Bob found seas of ants crowded next to the tiniest dropped crumbs and I saw a large rat, not easily confused with a mongoose, at the regularly overflowing garbage drop-off. None of these things discouraged us from our plans.

My husband decided we needed to buy a copy of the local telephone book. The purchase was quite an introduction to the daily rhythms of on-island living. We learned that formal politeness is expected for the most minor personal interactions, that patience is a mandatory skill set for daily survival and that persistence is important to accomplish ones goals. Our adventure went like this:

Bob and I went to 'Connections' where everything on-island seems to center. Inside this tiny business, there was a wall where jobs and apartment ads were posted, private phone booths were for rent and faxes and telegrams could be sent or received. A large clock on one wall was labeled "Grand Central" with the local time and a row of clocks lining the opposite wall were accurate for Tokyo, Paris, London and so on. Bob pointed out one clock in the row titled "Coral Bay" which was the tiny settlement on the other side of the island.

This clock had no clock hands. "Pretty accurate," I smiled. Coral Bay was the most laid back and quiet place I'd ever been.

The nice ladies at Connections said phone books could only be gotten at the Vitelco (VI Telephone Company) office, which was located in a small trailer parked down the street. At the Vitelco office, Bob and I waited patiently for our turn. When it came, Bob asked if we could buy a phonebook. We were sent to a corner of the room with a disgruntled "wait". Three people behind us were then serviced first, while we tried to determine what he'd said to cause such unhappiness. It dawned on me that everyone else began their conversation by saying 'Good Day' and then waiting for a response and a query of what their business was. Aha.

I whispered this thought to Bob and when we were finally waived back to the reception desk he tried this technique. This time his greeting was met with a broad smile, and then success - we could indeed buy a phone book for a very reasonable price, but they could not accept cash or a personal check and told us to come back with a money order.

We went back to Connections but this time a smiling face redirected us to the U.S. Post Office. There we stood in line for what seemed like an eternity before our turn came. Bob and I made the most of that time chatting with others in line and learning the fine art of patience. Those who were the most serene were the 'professionals' - those who earned their living standing in line for other businesses and making a tidy profit for the pain. It took us twice through the line before we were done, as we hadn't filled out the prerequisite form in advance. With our money order finally in hand, Bob and I went back to Vitelco only to find out that the telephone book would be mailed to us in a week.

Ah, patience. Six weeks later, it arrived in our Massachusetts mailbox.

I talked with seemingly everyone on St. John about daily island life. Special efforts were made to speak to working-class folks, especially those who didn't seem to be in jobs that would make them rich. When we moved to this Paradise, we'd likely be a part of this crowd. Waitresses and store clerks and artists and construction workers all contributed their thoughts. While some encouraged and others discouraged our dreams, I began to get a solid understanding of the differences we'd face.

Their stories were amazing. They confirmed that anyone could make it here if they really wanted to, single mothers with children, and even whole families. Most people were happy. One thing that struck me was the number of people who'd gotten divorced once they'd been here for a while. The main reason given was that the ex-spouse didn't share their vision of Paradise. Alcohol abuse was next on the list, which made sense in a place where rum is cheaper than Kool-Aid.

Bob and I returned home from that Thanksgiving vacation on St. John with new resolve. Before it waned a few weeks later, the local USVI phone book arrived, along with our new subscription to the St. John biweekly newspaper. Another notebook had been filled with insights gleaned from our travels. These investments proved invaluable over the following year. Every two weeks, when the *Tradewinds* newspaper was due in our mailbox, I tried to beat Bob home to ensure I got a chance to read it first. That newspaper had become a tangible link to our future home and Bob tended to hoard.

Businesses occasionally advertised on computer Internet sites that I then researched for more information. I kept these sessions to myself, feeling I'd gone a little overboard in looking for the smallest St. John news tidbits. That winter I discovered that while I was quietly researching the Internet at night, Bob had been doing the same thing in the early morning hours. It became a game of sorts to find a new Web site with previously unknown information that might be useful to share with each other.

Home projects at our residence in New England plagued us. Like most homeowners, we'd put off so many things that we had a home fix-up and improvement list five pages long. It was important to get the house into saleable shape. The home sale was critical to funding our dream. Our neighbors still didn't believe our plans and one suggested that these projects were part of an unconscious nesting instinct on our part. They couldn't accept we were ready for a migration. The floors were refinished, built-in cabinets added in the upstairs bedrooms, and walls everywhere got a fresh coat of paint. The list of home improvements needed initially grew faster than the projects could be completed.

For the first time in a long time, Bob and I read newspaper inserts, looking for sales for tools and building materials and then for decorative items to fit with the new room looks. Just a few inexpensive purchases and some creativity were all that were needed to give each room a special look. After the clutter of ages had been removed. It took a full basement and two yard sales to make it all work, but the results were pleasing.

As an extravagance, Bob bought an inexpensive ceiling fan and had it installed in what passed for the master bedroom. The room, with it's unevenly slanted walls, was painted a bright glossy white against the advice of almost everyone. With the hardwood floor newly refinished and a couple of inexpensive palm plants tucked into corners, the room all of a sudden had a distinctively Caribbean feel. When I added an old Bentwood rocker and removed all the personal clutter, it was impressive. Instantly, it became our favorite room.

The Holiday season had always been a big deal in our home. . There were still mounds of presents for each other, but the tone of the gifts changed. We bought things each other had been privately wanting, but had been living without. An expensive bottle of Scotch and luxury food items made their way into wrapping paper. We jointly ordered a subscription to *The VI Daily News*, a daily newspaper from St. Thomas. Gifts that were practical, but fun, were the best. My favorite was a mosquito net that added just the right effect to our Caribbean style bedroom and which might be useful on St. John.

Our St. John vacation over Thanksgiving had convinced us to reconsider our planned timing for the move. With the current timetable, we'd be moving at the beginning of tourist season less than two years out. We knew what that meant, since we'd just visited during that time of year. It just wasn't practical. Housing would be hard to find, and everything would be at a premium price. With the added tourist influx and our lack of local knowledge, it would be difficult to distinguish us from the crowd. Often tourists are smitten with the island on their visits. Too often they are unprepared for daily life and go back to the mainland after a few months. Potential landlords and employers are always wary of new transplants from the mainland, especially during the winter tourist season. We were determined to be long-term residents who would overcome the odds.

It was more logical to move months later, once the winter tourist season was over. We'd been saving to cover our expenses for the first year without any income, so the lack of jobs off-season were of minor concern. Fewer people meant we'd have time to settle into the rhythm of the island more easily. Once we had housing Bob and I could search for jobs and with luck we'd find some before tourist season started. It was rational and it was logical. But it wasn't palatable to either of us.

That cold February, the thought of adding six months to our schedule prior to the move was depressing. But the idea of moving six months earlier than our plan dictated seemed impossible unless a miracle occurred. I was anxious to get there but doubted we could reach our financial goals in little over a year, to accommodate a quicker move. A convenient blizzard sapped both our energies and we put off the decision for a few days that turned into months.

We should have started much sooner getting subscriptions to the island newspapers. The wealth of research information was amazing. Ads for groceries, cable TV, household goods and restaurants helped me define a realistic monthly budget. My friend Birdie browsed through The *VI Daily News* one Wednesday - I'd told her this was the 'food' day for the paper with supermarket ads, etc. She wryly commented that she should do her 'sale' shopping on St. Thomas instead of central New Hampshire, as the prices appeared cheaper, at least for some items. Her perspective was flawed since the 'non-sale' items are generally a good bit higher than in the States. Still, it made our budgets more promising.

Bob and I became frugal in every way. I almost always used coupons at the local supermarket. We tried hard to only buy only what we needed and also to buy only what was on sale. Bob had begun washing our cars at home rather than at the car wash. We pumped our own gas. I remembered family folk lore that said my grandmother used to clean and reuse old foil wrap and plastic and saved discarded string for some useful future. She seldom threw anything out without it having five lives first. We'd become my grandmother.

For Bob's birthday, I bought a topographical map set of the Virgin Islands and a solar battery re-charger. I'd received summer clothing and a Caribbean cookbook for my own birthday. Other indiscriminate shopping had stopped. Our once twice-weekly restaurant forays had become history, and our lives became simplified. I wondered when my life had become so cluttered with 'things'. Had I ever really been that young college girl who traveled through Europe for a month with just one small duffel bag?

The truth is, we'd been pack rats for years. I'm convinced Bob was born that way. Our pantry had always been full - Bob insisted on having not one but three backup bottles of laundry detergent - just in case. Add this to the extra canned goods, garden supplies, garage paraphernalia and every other household item one can imagine and it was evident we had a long way to go before considering ourselves 'free spirits'. It took us a long time to wean ourselves even temporarily from these habits. While depleting these extraordinary supplies, our 'necessity' shopping slowed down while our savings account soared.

Our pack rat tendencies were not limited to household supplies. I had clothes that I'd never worn and probably never would. My closets and the linen closet were attacked with a vengeance that resulted in a rag pile that resembled a small mountain. Bob's collection of screen-printed clothing from past kayaking events was considered off limits, but a drawer full of unopened new underwear spoke volumes. A threat to throw the whole drawer into the rag pile got most new items unpacked and into use. I sneakily snitched his old underwear to add to the rag mountain.

Nothing in our lives was immune to our paring down of material possessions. Bob was in a terrible quandary. He had too many toys and since he'd find little whitewater in the Caribbean, the right thing to do was to sell his backup whitewater kayak. The money could be put aside for a possible sea kayak sometime down the road. Parting with his battered beginners kayak was an emotional issue though it hadn't been used in years. The day Bob sold it to a good home was a defining moment. Bob's resulting depression lasted only a day, which brought a big sigh of relief from me. Despite the fact that he still owned a newer kayak, no friend ever again questioned his commitment to Paradise.

We painted the house that spring, deciding on a pleasant blue that we felt was more harmonious than the drab green we'd lived with for years. The trim would be a darker blue, and with the inevitable white trim on the windowsills and doors, it would be reminiscent of the colorful homes on St. John with their multi-colored trims. Was it ever! The color we selected for the main color dried a brighter color than we'd expected. After a couple of days, Bob and I got used to it, and decided we'd keep the color. It had grown on us, and felt like a little Caribbean spot right in the middle of New England. When the project was nearly complete, I spied a neighbor across the back yard, working in his garden.

"So what do you think of our new paint job?" I hailed over the dividing stone wall.

"Pat," he called to his wife over his shoulder. "Get my sunglasses. I can't see who's calling me with all that BLUE over there!" he chuckled.

"It's not THAT blue," I threw back at him, but I knew he had a point. My neighbor just chuckled louder.

From that day till now, our old homestead is known as the "Blue Place". It may have been a little too Caribbean for New England, but it fit its owners' moods that spring. With my USVI vanity plate on my car, our intentions were clear to the whole world.

Spring cleaning also meant a comprehensive review of our financial status. I pulled out the notebooks and the mounds of backup data, and got down to work. Imagine my surprise when I discovered that we were saving at a rate equaling over 53% of our net income! Two years earlier Bob and I had been saving at a combined rate less than 5%! And, neither my husband nor myself had denied ourselves any item we truly wanted or needed. I did the numbers three times looking for errors. We were closer to our goal than we'd known. It had paid to be conservative for once.

At the back of my mind, I kept coming back to the thought of moving to St. John six months earlier than planned. Could it be done? Bob had abdicated the budgetary planning to me. He was sure I could figure it out. I was sure I couldn't. An unexpected phone call from Juneau, Alaska helped me make the decision. Our friends had just passed another long dark winter in their version of Paradise. Their enthusiasm for their adopted home was infectious. They'd never been within thousands of miles of St. John, but they shared our passion. Their parting words of advice were inspiring.

"If it's right, it will work out, no matter what. Just pick a date and maybe next year this time you'll be in your own Paradise."

These parting words stuck with me throughout the day as I reworked the budgets and played with the timetable. By evening, I shyly suggested a revised timeline to Bob. He was excited to say the least. Totally out of character, he called numerous friends that night to share the news.

"I've been reworking the numbers and I've picked a date to move . . . " he started every conversation. I was so pleased by his excitement that I forgot to be annoyed that Bob took credit for it all.

Paradise would be our home four short seasons from now. We were doing it less than three years from our backyard pact to move to Paradise within ten years. There was no turning back.

We were solidly committed.

Chapter Three
Out With The Old

With commitment firmly in hand, we faced a sad task. Our home needed to be sold - soon. Spring and early summer were the best times to show off the beauty of the property, and we had no idea if we'd sell quickly once we put it on the market. Our plans couldn't risk the burden of a mortgage when we were ready for the move to Paradise. We expected to sell the house at a loss, but if we were lucky, the loss would be minimal. Waiting was too risky.

If we could have, we'd have taken our whole neighborhood with us when we moved. It was that good a neighborhood. I would especially miss watching all the local children grow up without me.

From our vantage point, the house was ready to be sold. Most of the home improvements had been completed, and it looked darned good. The late spring flower bulbs had blossomed and the yard was filled with the color and sweet smells that promised a long summer. Neighborhood kids occasionally trekked through our yard with their bikes or just to visit for a while. Unfortunately, we were enjoying living there more than at any time in our past. Nostalgia was everywhere.

Because of a new State law, our septic system needed replacing before our home sale could be completed. Bob took over this arduous task, managing all of the contractors and agencies it entailed. It was my job to find a realtor. I'd met a wonderful one a year earlier when she stopped by on an old bicycle at one of our yard sales. Warm and charming, she'd displayed good taste too, buying a small braided rug I missed dearly. With a smile she'd given me her business card and said, "call me if you're ever looking for an agent". It was an invitation with no pressure or expectation attached. Miraculously, I still had her card. A phone call was all it took - she vividly remembered my yard sale and our home. We held our breaths waiting for her visit and her verdict.

The house was proclaimed 'ready' despite the septic work to be done and a price was suggested. I gulped, but agreed - it was a realistic but generous price compared to similar properties selling in our area. We would definitely be selling at a loss, but wouldn't lose too much. The real estate agent was amazed at the work we'd done and smiled in agreement with the improvements Bob had decided weren't neces-sary. She actually liked the bright blue color of our home. We'd found our broker.

With honesty she warned us that with summer around the corner, it was unlikely the property would sell before fall. We were prepared. Secretly, I was glad. It meant enough time to get the new septic system installed and we'd get to stay until it was at least time to rake the leaves for one last time. It wasn't that I had cold feet - but our home in summer was magical. The next day, I began planting my last vegetable garden and my last flower garden. The flowers were especially important to me, since for over five years I'd dabbled in various floral crafts. By now I'd become skilled and would enjoy the endeavor. There'd be time to grow, dry and sell floral bouquets for one last season. Two weeks later the property was on the market.

Imagine our surprise when the property went under contract in less than one week on the market. The price was right, and we got lucky. The family that bought our home had been ready to buy once before when a final home inspection came out negative. Their humble goals were a large yard and a big master bedroom and a place their only son would love. Bingo! Our neighbors "interviewed" these folks - or let's just say they were very inquisitive - to both realtors' horror on the second walk-through of the property. Everything fell into place. The little boy made fast friends with the entire neighborhood that afternoon and when the adults started sharing soft drinks and beer, it was a done deal in everyone's minds. Bob and I sat on the swing, stunned.

From that day on, our summer was frantic.

The law required that the new septic system be installed and completed before the sale could go through. The home closing would be at the end of August - months before we'd expected. There were still huge amounts of accumulated 'junk' we owned that weren't practical to take to a short-term apartment rental. And what about the garden crops? And where would we go? Our friends and family were united in their belief that Bob and I were crazy.

Advice from the naysayers had had their impact. We'd settled on St. John as the ultimate Paradise, but our research had been rather incomplete. While we'd spent time on nearby St. Thomas during each of our St. John vacations, we'd never visited St. Croix - called by some the Quiet Virgin. St. Croix is almost fifty miles south of St. John and while tourist literature described St. Thomas as urban and St. John as rural, they said St. Croix was suburban. St. Thomas was ruled out in our minds. While it was a wonderful place, there were too many people to suit us. Our Massachusetts home was a short thirty-minute ride to downtown Boston, yet we visited there only a couple of times per year. Besides, we might have to commute to St. Thomas if jobs were scarce and then we'd need the serenity of St. John for our sanity.

Housing on St. Croix was much more reasonably priced than St. John. We felt we had to make a visit before finalizing our plans. Bob had met a couple on the Internet, who'd moved to St. Croix a few months earlier from New England. George and Lisa were convinced that St. Croix was Paradise, so we hedged our bet on St. John and made a quick unscheduled trip to visit their island.

We easily found an inexpensive hotel to stay in downtown Christianstaad. Leaving the overseeing of our septic system replacement to our friend Dan, we headed south. Our cats went on their own vacation to Birdie's house. By the time we'd arrived at our hotel on St. Croix, we had three separate messages waiting for us. Two were for job possibilities that Internet friends had come up with, and the third was an invitation for dinner and drinks from George and Lisa.

The next night at dinner, George and Lisa were generous in sharing their experience in moving and their changed lives on the island. They'd rented a condo sight unseen, which seemed unthinkable to us. Within a few months on-island both were working in new fields, but with old skill sets. They candidly answered our many questions without a second thought. We learned how get our cars over on a barge from the mainland, how to register an automobile, and how to cook local vegetables. George and Lisa had never visited St. John, but St. Croix was good enough for them.

St. Croix was a wonderful island. It was much larger than St. John and had miles of gently sloping farmland along with the steep mountain roads that are a St. John hallmark. There were real shopping centers like on St. Thomas, but everything was more spread out. Everywhere we saw glimpses of St. Croix's proud history in its restored buildings and museums and other landmarks. The people we met were all warm and friendly and there was a camaraderie that was quickly comfortable.

Our vacation did not all go smoothly, but then again, we didn't have high expectations. Within twenty-four hours our rental car was broken into, the would-be thief disappointed there were no valuables in the car. The rental agent had forgotten to warn us not to lock the doors since this encouraged would be thieves. Bob and I didn't discuss this incident until a long time after it happened. We were both trying to give St. Croix fair consideration and we also didn't want to influence each others decision.

This trip combined typical vacation activities along with more practical ones. We went swimming and snorkeling but the inevitable comparison to beaches St. John provided expectations that were difficult to match. Bob and I visited a Social Security office to get new cards, as our new friends said we'd need original cards for various purposes once we moved. We met with potential employers and found concrete job opportunities on St. Croix within three days. I spent time in the grocery stores verifying prices and we discussed our plans and thoughts of moving with many people we met and unlike St. John, everyone was encouraging.

St. Croix appeared to be still struggling to recover from the effects of Hurricane Hugo many years ago. More recent hurricanes had stalled recovery and it seemed to me that many had lost confidence along with their homes. Still, it was an island of great potential. Real estate was surprisingly inexpensive. If St. Croix could begin to believe in itself again, any investment would bring large returns.

Our vacation coincided with the Summer Olympics being held in Atlanta. Between other activities and every night we'd return to our room and watch the events unfold. Neither Bob nor I talked much about our individual island observations or opinions. We were each a little afraid of what the other person thought. But during commercials, we each took out notebooks and summarized what we'd learned that day.

With only three days left to go before this vacation ended, it was time to bring matters to a head. During an extraordinarily long commercial while watching the Olympics, I broached the subject.

"So what do you think?" I finally asked.

"Well, we could easily live here," Bob said, which didn't really answer the question at all. I hoped a soft approach would get him to open up.

"It does seem like we'd fit in and have jobs pretty quick," I agreed.

After a short pause Bob added, "And we'd have a support group already in place to help us get settled." I knew he was thinking of George and Lisa who dined with us again the night before.

"But is this what you really want?" I pushed.

His next words were almost whispered. "It's not St. John." That was an understatement. I'd tried hard not to compare the two islands during this trip, but it was an impossible task. I nodded in agreement as he continued.

"But our money would last longer, and everything is less expensive than St. John." Ah, this was getting to the crux of the matter. And Bob was right. We could move to St. Croix immediately and be on budget with the money we'd already saved.

"True," I said with more perkiness in my voice than I felt. I hoped this wasn't Bob's way of telling me his decision had changed to St. Croix. So I held my breath for what came next.

"But, it's not what we've been saving for," he finally commented.

I quickly agreed. "We've been preparing to be poor. This would be so much easier," I said, hoping I wasn't actually convincing him.

"You're right - but being poor is fine if we're in Paradise." When he said these words, my hope soared.

"This isn't Paradise." I had to be blunt. It's what I felt.

"Not mine, anyway," Bob said, as the Olympic theme music began to signal the beginning of the next show segment.

"Maybe we should *Go For The Gold,*" I said with sudden inspiration.

"St. John is definitely the *Gold,*" Bob answered, still lost in his own thoughts. I doubt he even heard my reply when I agreed. After a few moments of silence, my husband turned to me and smiled. "Then let's *Go For The Gold.*"

Was it coincidence? At that very moment, the Olympic theme music blared again in earnest, signaling another commercial break. In unison we began humming the Olympic theme "Nah - Nah, nah-Nah-nah-Nah-nah". And so we sealed our fates.

Our last days on St. Croix were fond ones. We decided to wait and tell our new friends of our decision by e-mail once we got home. If nothing else, we'd be neighbors of sorts and maybe we could visit them for Carnival and they could do the same.

Rejuvenated from the trip, Bob and I came home to a frenzy of packing and cleaning. The closing date on the house got moved up a week to mid-August and we had nowhere to move. We still had three yard sales ahead of us. And the gardens were growing slower than normal - it looked like the new owners would get most of the harvest. While we were away, the town Health Inspector had decided that the only place the new septic system could go was under the old concrete patio directly behind our house. The buyers insisted that the patio be replaced, as close to its original condition as possible. And before the home closing. Of course.

To say we survived those last couple of months at our little homestead 'with a little help from our friends' would be a gross understatement. Neighbors and friends from miles away all offered their assistance along with their wisdom on even small matters. Offers to store household possessions, help with yard work, board our cats on occasion, and even to clean and bring in the harvest were given. Neighborhood parties on the weekends brought us all together but would make parting more difficult.

I was charged with selling off most of our belongings. Bob was in charge of whining about the things we were selling. But even he agreed with my philosophy on what things to keep. I'd taken a class long ago on Creative Thinking where I'd learned that a chair is only a chair if and when you use it as a chair. It could also be a table or a cage or even firewood, depending on how you use it. This was the wisdom we applied to deciding which items we must keep. We couldn't take everything - the moving budget wouldn't allow it. Multiuse items would be ideal since we expected to be living in a smaller place and we'd learned most long term rentals on St. John came furnished. Some of the things we kept would be considered bizarre by the uninitiated.

Selling all of our furniture now made sense, but we'd need to keep some pieces until moving to St. John, since we'd be living in an apartment locally for at least eight months before moving to Paradise. We opted to sell most things and live 'if we had to' with a portable camptable and lawn chairs in our temporary kitchen. It was a sure sign of our strong commitment to the future. Our two cats would not be able to go outdoors when we moved to a temporary apartment - it was too risky. I'm sure they sensed this. One insisted on staying outdoors that summer and the other cat was always perched near a window.

The yard sales were progressively eccentric, as we worked frantically to eliminate our excesses. We'd had two yard sales the previous year, but nothing like this. I was absolutely amazed by the interest displayed by the professional buyers. And although I should have been immune by this point, I was continuously stunned by some of the items people would pay money for at yard sales. Some items that went fast had been purchased at such sales myself over the years - confirming my good tastes in the eclectic. But we also sold weird stuff like used wine corks, little bottles of hotel shampoo, and old pieces of macramé.

Selling our home in summer meant the lawn and shrubs needed to be maintained in pristine shape, while we had less time than normal to address this time-consuming task. Our property included three quarters of an acre of manicured lawn and gardens that required constant work. Bob became a weekend warrior in keeping weeds at bay. His tasks were made more difficult by the septic system installation going on in the middle of it all. Mountains of dirt and strewn rocks combined with a dug up patio to provide constant havoc.

The crew Dan hired to help out did a commendable job. Every slab of concrete was identified and numbered to its exact location to ensure refitting later. This was especially necessary since the patio was made up of poured concrete slabs of differing sizes and shapes all pieced together in an exacting way to form the curved edges that eased the eye as it moved to the green lawn and gardens beyond. Keeping dirt and dust out of the house was a big challenge. We'd never owned an air conditioner and the fans we used in summer months to keep the kitchen area cool now pulled in great quantities of dust.

My Massachusetts job required occasional trips out of town. That summer, spousal trust would come into play for many decisions. The task of finding temporary living quarters fell solely on Bob's capable shoulders. It would not be easy, with two cats in tow and an unbending vow not to sign a one-year lease. He also owned the myriad of other moving tasks, like sending out mail forwarding forms and scheduling utility shutdowns and phone number transfers. Bob was a junk mail junkie, and I could only hope for the best - or worst.

We packed those things we were taking with us with little regard for the move next year. Eight months would give us plenty of time to fine tune the items we were taking with us. The rest would be donated to charity or thrown out. Friends had already spoken for a couple of items like our beds and a bookcase. We'd given one bed away with the caveat that we'd use it to sleep on when we visited New England. It was a creative way to be charitable to a good friend who had a lot of pride but not much money.

On warm summer evenings, I visited the gardens, picking the blooms for pressing and drying along with the occasional vegetable for dinner. Tending the gardens had always been a kind of therapy, mellowing me out after a stressful day at work. Whenever a flower came into full bud in the drying garden, I'd snap the bude off the stem and toss it into my harvest basket. Bob called it my 'sadistic' garden and I must admit I sometimes conjured up faces of those who didn't believe we would make it to St. John.

Since we would be gone before the full harvest was in, every little flower mattered. Each evening I would poke wires through flower buds and dry these in our cellar, which was crowded or empty depending on the time between yard sales. The dehumidifier was on constantly in hopes of speeding the drying process while the buds slowly bloomed on wired stems. That last month, Birdie would descend on a weekly basis, graciously taking the dried bouquets to her home to keep until the fall crafts fair season.

Suddenly, it was over. We'd slept our last night in sleeping bags in the master bedroom, with potted palm trees for company on the hard floor. The new owners had liked the room so much that they'd even bought the plants. We were moving out in the morning, although the closing wasn't until the following week. My work and travel schedule was volatile, so we had gotten all to agree to have the closing without us. That last morning, my husband and I sat on our patio swing looking out at the back yard. The gardens were just getting to their prime and a cat was lounging comfortably overhead soaking up the warm morning sun as Bob sat, lost in thought.

"This is it," I said. But the only response was silence.

"We're really doing it," I tried again, with much the same result. Maybe sentimentality would get Bob to open up. "I'm going to miss everybody," I suggested, but even this had no effect. So I sat and brooded.

"Everything will change." I must have said this out loud, because to my surprise, my husband answered my thought.

"Life is change. Change is good." That was all he said as he continued to gaze on our former home.

"Let's go find our temporary abode," I said, hoping Bob was right.

St. John Trivia

All the beaches on St. John are considered public property by law, from the low tide line to either the line of vegetation or fifty feet inland, whichever is the shorter distance. However, public access by land is not mandated, which keeps some beaches secreted from most tourists. Others are hidden by lush foliage and steep hillsides.

There are thirty-nine accessible beaches on St. John, but most tourists visit only the beaches at Trunk Bay, Cinnamon Bay or Hawksnest Bay on the north shore, which are easily reached by open-air taxis.

Chapter Four
Living in Hell

Up front, I have to admit we didn't handle the move from our house to our apartment very well. But the quick move from the apartment to the condo went much smoother. It's a sad saga...

I'd never been to the new apartment before. We got there around noon that Sunday, following the trucks our friends had volunteered to carry the bulk of our possessions. Our cats had been farmed out to Birdie for a couple of weeks to simplify our move. With the promise of only free food, we received near professional assistance from our mover friends. Soon we were there.

Millions of people have lived in an almost identical apartment. It was a corner two-bedroom unit on the bottom floor of a huge three-story building complex. There was a swimming pool we'd maybe use twice before we'd move again, and parking all around the building. I'd lived in a similar place over twenty years ago. Even my husband had lived in its twin before he knew me.

It appeared that Bob had played it safe when it came to apartment hunting. The complex belonged to a large property management company in the region. Our building was directly across the parking lot from the rental office with its model apartments for prospective renters. Because we were on the ground floor, most items were simply brought in through the sliding glass doors separating living room from the small concrete enclosed patio.

We moved more things than we needed, including some potted tomato plants and flowers still in bud, to cheer up the place. As a big picture frame was placed to lean against the wall on top of a stack of boxes, Birdie saw and killed an errant bug. She made a little joke about the bug being a new neighbor, but I gave the comment little thought. I was busy directing the small army of men carrying boxes to and fro, was tired and in no mood for frivolity. Bob had inspected the apartment during a lunch break from work the previous week and the rental paperwork we'd been given said the apartment was in "move in" condition. By two o'clock we were moved in, just twenty minutes away from our old home.

Birdie stayed a little longer than the others to help me settle in, while I sent Bob off for a couple of hours with his buddies. She used my new dishwasher then filled an open cabinet with clean dishes. By sunset, Birdie was gone, leaving my husband and myself to our new apartment. As we had often done at our house, I heated some water to make us each a cup of tea. When I opened the cabinet where the cleaned dishes were kept, I let out a screech.

"Roaches!" There were cockroaches scurrying everywhere. There were even roaches climbing into the newly cleaned cups. I ran into the small living room.

"Show me," Bob said in disbelief as he followed me back to the kitchen. "There's some in the sink now," he screeched as he opened a drawer and more rushed for cover against the sudden light.

I was thoroughly disgusted. I HATED cockroaches. Yes, I know there are many in Paradise. Yes, I know there are 'really big ones'. But, I still hated them and I didn't expect to have to deal with them until we moved to the Caribbean. Besides, living in New England, we were hardly prepared for an infestation. Bob did his best to calm me down and downplay the situation. He called the property management office, while I sat out on the patio, feeling much safer there. The person who answered the phone told Bob nothing could be done until the office reopened the next day. We were stuck there for the night.

Bob turned lights on all over the apartment to keep any other cockroaches in hiding. He coaxed me inside after a few hours and convinced me there were none in the bedroom. Meanwhile he'd moved some essentials back into our cars to hedge his bet. Maybe I'd overreacted, but I was tired and stressed out. Exterminators would come in the morning and the cockroaches would be history. I refused to go into the kitchen or even the bathroom that night, but I did go to bed. Sleep was a long time coming.

Despite misgivings, we both went to work the next day. No exterminators came. A note on our doorway from the exterminating company said the premises were to be fumigated the next day, Tuesday. Having found more live cockroaches that very morning in the living room and the bathroom, I was paranoid. Fumbling, I opened the door only a crack, reached into the apartment, and turned on a light. I prayed this would eventually make the little pests run and scatter where I wouldn't have to see them. Then I went out to the apartment building steps to wait for Bob. When he arrived, we sat and we deliberated.

Bob came up with a creative solution for an interim living solution. We'd sleep at our old home in sleeping bags he'd packed in the car the previous night. The house was still ours for a few days. Thank goodness for camping vacations, because we were prepared to 'rough it'. We vacated the premises. In fact, we decided to give the new apartment an extra day or two after fumigation before setting foot in it. This would provide extra time to do final cleaning at the old house, which still faced our weary souls. It was a plan, but it didn't work.

I got out of work early that Friday and rushed to the new apartment to get it aired out a little before the sun set. Taped to the door was the exterminator's note verifying that the work had been done. I opened the door and the smell from the fumigation process was very strong. I pulled the protective plastic covering off of the bed mattress and opened the screened windows. The clean linens I'd brought with me were spread on the bed. Then I went out to my car to get pillows and blankets. When I returned from the parking lot and entered the bedroom, I thought I'd lost my mind.

There was a large, very alive cockroach crawling across the bed sheet I'd just placed down minutes ago. Another was on the wall in front of me. I flew out of the room. There was another scurrying across the living room wall and another one running to safety between the couch cushion and it's frame. I didn't scream this time. I was too grossed out even for that. By the time I'd gathered my senses, I'd already taken the phone out to the patio. I called the property management office. Their answering service told me they were closed but I insisted on talking to SOMEBODY immediately. I finally got to someone in security that told me there was nothing he could do until the office opened the next morning. No amount of hysteria would change this. He promised to fumigate again the next morning.

Bob was out of town until Sunday. He was blissfully kayaking at the annual Merrimack Valley Paddler's Pig Roast Weekend and couldn't be reached. I called Birdie - and asked if I could join my cats in bunking at her place.

Being such a dear friend, Birdie told me to come immediately. I hadn't been coherent enough to explain what happened - just that Bob was out of town and I needed a place to sleep. She knew something bad had happened, but she didn't push. By the time I traveled the thirty minutes to her home, Birdie had a bottle of wine and some snacks ready and the couch made up as a bed. It was to be home for two nights.

The drive back to the complex that Sunday morning gave me time to focus on the previous week. On a hunch, I went to the apartment first. Walking in, I saw no sure sign this latest fumigation had taken place - but I did see lots of cockroaches - mostly dead and but some very alive. It was like they'd completely taken over the apartment. There were literally thousands - in hindsight, I wish I had taken a photograph. I ran halfway across the parking lot to the management office before I realized where I was, somehow gripping a cordless telephone from the apartment. By this point, I was angry - very angry. The receptionist tried to placate me.

"Yes, I know who you are. We've never had roaches before in this complex, so we've been awfully concerned... I know I would be a little flipped out too if it happened to me... I understand why you want to talk with someone... I'm sure there's just a few stragglers - it takes a few days for them to all die when we fumigate."

I didn't believe her - there were too many cockroaches everywhere for this to be a freak situation. She was just too calm for my peace of mind. I wanted a solution and I wanted it now. We'd already stayed away a week and were paying for an apartment we couldn't even live in.

I demanded a temporary place to live - one that was cockroach free - and demanded to see someone in charge. I was told to sit and wait. A polo shirted man bearing the management company logo came in and tried to minimize the situation. He suggested that in a day or two they would be able to come up with an alternative apartment. It would be on a second floor, not great for our cats, but it was ours for the asking.

After sleeping on a floor for days, then a couch and hardly sleeping at all in fear the night before all that, I was in no mood for compromises. My agitated state and blunt response must have had an impact. Again I was told to wait. Within minutes the man returned saying there was a furnished one bedroom apartment on the third floor of our own building 3

Together, we went to our infested apartment to get some items. We needed clean clothes for the next workday at a minimum. I'd left a couple of lights on, which helped. We rushed through the apartment grabbing what we needed and tried not to notice a couple of scurrying shapes. Quickly, we rushed upstairs and out to the small deck outside the temporary quarters, where we dropped the things we'd collected. In the late afternoon sun, Bob picked up each item one by one, giving each a thorough look and good shake before bringing it inside. There were no cockroaches on these few items. The procedure was repeated twice, though the last load stayed outside on the deck overnight. We were dead tired.

The next day, our jobs kept us away and the day went too slowly. By the time I'd gotten to the apartment complex, Bob had cleared out the deck and was bringing up a new load of goods from the infested apartment. As he walked outside, I saw a very dead cockroach between the deck slats. It had probably come up with some of our possessions from the day before. I rushed into the kitchen and quickly pulled open drawers and cabinets. No cockroaches. In every room I repeated this action just to be sure.

There was nothing. I was relieved. We could beat this thing. With renewed vigor, we emptied the contents of boxes Bob had retrieved onto the deck and searched for little critters. Bob had bought many canisters of roach repellent during his lunch break that we used freely. Unfortunately most of our precious possessions were still downstairs getting more infested with every day that passed.

We lived by the moment for the next couple of days. Neither wanted to live in this complex any more but we needed to find somewhere else to live fast. We looked through the apartment rentals, and circled any that looked remotely hopeful. Phone calls nixed quite a few places. On Saturday we spent the day looking at apartments and filling out applications. No one could commit an answer until Monday when our applications were reviewed.

In the Saturday paper, there appeared some new ads. One was for a condo on the opposite side of town, and sounded perfect. I tried not to get my hopes up, as I circled other places for a Sunday hunt. Bob had already reached his limits - guilt over his original apartment selection combined with the hard work and little sleep from the previous two weeks had caught up to him. I would look for a new place the next day while he would take the day off and go kayaking for maybe the last time. It worked for both of us.

That Sunday I saw three more apartments and got lost looking for a fourth. The second one was the condo on the other side of town that sounded too perfect to be true. It was located just off a highway entrance, but as I drove there, I saw it was far enough away that the only sounds coming through my car windows were those of the birds in the nearby trees. Nestled in a quiet residential area of single family homes, the complex had much appeal. The condo unit itself was one in a long row, separated only by the long shrub-lined driveway that led down from the road above. It was townhouse styled with a one-car garage underneath, two bedrooms and one and a half baths. Almost as large as the home we'd just sold, it was in immaculate condition.

The condo was over our budget, but not by too much. And the owner seemed to understand our need for urgency in the move. I'd filled out the requisite application and the owner seemed warm and friendly and reminded me of a kindly yet firm grandmother. We had to sign a one-year lease, though our plan to was to move to St. John in ten months. Still, it was the best living situation I'd seen and the place was clean. There was no way a cockroach had ever found it's way into this condo. I said a silent little prayer and gave her our work phone numbers. Then I went to my next appointment, just in case it didn't pan out.

Luckily, the following day the condo owner called with the sweet words that answered my prayers. We rushed over after work for her to meet Bob and show him how the central vacuum system worked since we'd never owned one. The increase in monthly rent faded in my mind. Before the day was over, we were ready to move in.

St. John Trivia

Long term rental properties on St. John always seem to be in high demand. In those rare instances where choices are available, the following are common questions locals ask before making their decision:

- *How badly will it rain inside the apartment when there's a rain shower outside?*

- *Will I need a 4-wheel drive vehicle to get to the apartment, and will I need a new transmission and brakes within 60 days?*

- *If it's in Cruz Bay, just how loud is the decibel level at 11PM on a Friday night? (Carnival time doesn't count)*

- *Is there a view of ANYTHING?*

- *Are there rooms bigger than the size of a bathtub?*

- *Is it screened in, or open and inviting to outside critters?*

- *How hot (sunny) and claustrophobic (like a cavern) will it be?*

- *How many goats, donkeys, roosters, pigs and dogs wander past the front door in a 24 hour period?*

- *How often does it run out of water, or if in Cruz Bay – just how grungy does the water come out of the faucet?*

- *How much personal property damage will result from a minimum-level hurricane, or worse, a mere tropical storm?*

- *Is the rent < 50% of my yearly income?*

Chapter Five
Living in Limbo

The condo was like a breath of fresh air after the cockroach-infested apartment from hell. It was months before I could laugh about the situation. Birdie was threatened with lifetime abandonment if she even mentioned the word "cockroach" in my presence for the next six months.

Within a day we'd moved in. Our mover friends had come to our rescue again. I wished I could have given them a medal or something. It meant that much. They moved us quickly, since the bed, living room couch and armchair had to be left behind. The cockroaches had had too much time to make new homes in our old furniture, and we were worried about health issues if we fumigated further. We'd planned to leave that furniture behind when we moved to Paradise but we faced reality bravely.

Even with the furniture and other items we'd lost to the cockroaches, we should have eliminated more things. The condo had more space than the apartment before but we later found we needed that space to sort, pack and stage items for shipping. In the beginning it seemed like wasted rent money for empty space.

Everything that had been in the apartment was put in the new garage. Before it went inside, a few canisters of roach spray covered every crack and seam. Afterwards, the entire garage was sprayed again. I was determined that not even one cockroach would survive the trip to the new condo.

Bob and I slept in our trusty sleeping bags. A blanket in the corner warmed the cats. These were the only items we had ready for the master bedroom. Two lawn chairs filled the living room, and the rest of the place was empty. Occasional forays were made to the garage for items that just couldn't wait. Our workdays seemed very long and our night activities were sparse. The garage was filled to the top with our remaining furniture, our 'toys' and boxes of every size and shape.

Whenever we opened the door we sealed it with roach spray before closing. A lamp was rescued for the bedroom and a pot for the kitchen. A week after the move, we began spending all of our free time rescuing and cleaning items one by one. From the amount of things that went into the dumpster, I'm convinced we threw out more than we brought inside.

Bob spent much time getting our mail situation straightened out. Moving twice in one month made this work frustrating and confusing. He grumbled but kept at it, while my back was getting more sore each day.

After two weeks of sleeping bags, I put my foot down. I wanted somewhere comfortable to sleep. And we needed some furniture in the living room, even if it was for only eight months. Eventually, he gave in, found a furniture outlet store and purchased an inexpensive sleeper-couch. It made a big difference. At least we were able to sleep somewhere other than the floor.

Our friend Dan loaned us a kitchen table with four matching chairs. He'd always had an extra key to our living space, for both his and our convenience, and the 'new' kitchen set was a wonderful surprise, already in the dining area and set up when I arrived home one day. We were now living in relative comfort with both a 'furnished' living/bed room and dining room. I began efforts to convince Bob to splurge further on a new mattress and box spring.

In the confusion of the past few weeks Bob and I had begun the very bad habit of eating fast food and other take-out meals on a constant basis. We were getting fat. It was time to find kitchen items and begin cooking. Cooking meant 'home' to me and once I started to cook on a regular basis both Bob and I began to relax into this phase of our existence. It also was the reason our kitchen got redecorated before anywhere else. "To add a few homey comforts and minimize the condo's sparseness" was the excuse I used while I weekly earmarked a small amount of money from my budgeted cash for this effort.

Looking back, it was worth it. I'd decided that the kitchen should be decorated in an 'island' motif using some items we'd bought during past vacations and using color to make it all work. The table Dan loaned us was an oak butcher-block one with four cane-seated chairs.

Above it was a colonial looking chandelier. I covered the chandelier with cheap plastic ivy plants and hung a little mobile of parrots we'd bought years ago on St. Thomas for a couple of dollars. The ivy theme got carried throughout the dining and kitchen areas. I later added a wooden parrot in a swing hanging above the sink, which Birdie and I picked up at a craft fair that fall. Island-style warmth radiated throughout.

Redecorating wasn't limited to the condo. My USVI license plate had fallen off my car at a car wash soon after our move so I decided to post it on my office wall as a conversation piece. By this time the thing was rather beat up. That made it even more endearing. It was a constant reminder of our plans and a response to the naysayers who were my closest office co-workers. What selling our home couldn't accomplish, the battered license plate did. Co-workers finally began to believe that Bob and I were serious about Paradise.

While they wondered about Paradise, Bob and I were still unpacking an endless pile of boxes. Ten months until our planned move date felt like a very long time. I hated the idea of paying rent money for the extra months on the lease, but I'd been brought up to accept responsibility and never skip town. Bob, always the wise one, told me to put it out of my mind and act like a St. Johnian and "go with the flow". I did, but only because the crafts fair season had already begun.

Despite our short summer at the old homestead, I'd managed to harvest a respectable amount of flowers. Birdie and I had been 'doing' crafts fairs for years, mostly for quality girl time alone and to enjoy some nice fall days outdoors. We never made any money to speak of, but we had fun times together. The schedule Birdie and I had agreed on was small - only three craft fairs - but still we weren't prepared. Birdie was 'retiring' at the end of the season. It just wouldn't be fun to pursue, she insisted, if we couldn't do it together. By the end of the last fair, we still had some items left. They would become Christmas presents and personal souvenirs to take to Paradise.

Our mail and our newspaper subscriptions caught up with us after a few short weeks of confusion. On days when we didn't receive *The VI Daily News* or the *Tradewinds* was overdue, both my husband and I felt let down. We'd come to depend on these links to our future home. Sometimes two or three papers arrived in one day, and sometimes none, as the weekly mail cycle ebbed and flowed. When we received a Friday's paper before we had received that Thursday's, it was a little quirk that reminded us both that St. John would not be perfect. While the news was always a few days old, it hardly mattered. Bob and I ate it up.

Most of our friends and family had finally adjusted to our moving to Paradise sometime soon. Advice and opinions flowed freely. My mother-in-law was very worried about our move to the Virgin Islands. Since we'd sold the house, there was no denying that we were really going. She kept us informed of every TV show and news clip she saw showing crime in the islands and hoping to discourage us. Her efforts amused us, but we also took them seriously.

She sent us a clipping of a long article about someone who had made the move to St. John but didn't last. We read it with great interest.

The writer's disillusionment didn't faze Bob or I, as we could easily tell the writer wasn't well prepared for island life. He wasn't adaptable to life outside of a city, or one without lots of conveniences. The article was reaffirming. There was a two-column insert titled 'If You're Planning To Go' that had recommendations for research to do first. We'd already bought and read the books and had subscribed to the newspaper. Surely, we were ready for the realities of the big move.

My own parents' approach was a little different. I could tell my mother thought our plan a pipe dream and not something we were really going to do. Despite selling our house. She would express great interest in plans for the move. Then she'd inevitably laugh and say we were crazy and end our conversations with "Well, Honey, you should go for it if you want it". It was spring before she was convinced we were really going. My father attempted to assess our success potential in a more circumspect manner. He regularly asked Bob if he was as excited about moving as I am. I'm sure my dad was thinking about my first marriage and the move that portended disaster. Bob always answered him in the affirmative, but he's so quiet by nature, it never came out sounding enthusiastic.

That Halloween, few children knocked on our door. I found myself anxious for the night to be over so I could pack away the very first of the boxes to be sent to our home in Paradise. I missed the children from our old neighborhood and I wondered what they were wearing for Halloween this year. We'd never spent Halloween on St. John and didn't know if it was a holiday that we'd be celebrating again.

The garage was finally empty enough to get a car in there, with some strong creativity on our part. Bob had suggested organizing remaining gear, like camping stuff, ski equipment, snow shovels, etceteras into sections along the walls, held up with nails. At least that stuff was off the ground and out of the way. It was also easy to retrieve even with a car parked in the garage.

That same day, Birdie called. She was throwing out all her craft supplies and gave me the option of taking whatever I wanted. It was my own fault. I was up to my eyeballs trying to clean out the garage and she wanted me to make decisions on things I couldn't see and couldn't take the time to figure out if I needed. So I said I'd take whatever she was throwing out. It was a mistake - the next day the garage looked like we'd never cleaned at all. The 'craft' stuff turned out to include lots of items I'd never seen before. I could only hope the garage would be empty by Christmas.

Some craft items would be useful to take to Paradise. Bob and I both wanted to explore more of our artistic abilities once in St. John. That meant bringing raw materials and other supplies with us. With no clue regarding the arts or crafts we wanted to try our hand at, I guessed at the right things. Research had told me it's difficult to acquire cheap supplies locally on the island. Of course there are wholesale catalogs, but only few items can be bought in enough quantity to be reasonably priced. Some items would be difficult to find at all.

My husband often beat me to the mailbox those days and once in a while, he'd forget to pass the USVI papers on to me. Eventually I learned about the first recently held 'St. John Saturday'. This event was to become a regular one, held once a month in Cruz Bay, including craft booths with local talent giving me my first on-island goal: to make handcrafts of good value to sell in my own booth on St. John Saturdays. For the rest of our tenure at the condo, when pictures of the monthly event arrived in the *Tradewinds*, I studied them in great detail.

Thanksgiving was spent with our immediate family and by then our lives were almost normal. In mid December, word of an incident in Paradise soured our mood. We'd gotten the latest *Tradewinds* newspaper and read it through as usual, noting the issue had a negative tone throughout. An article about panhandlers was prominent and made St. John sound more like we'd seen on St. Croix. There was another article about two people who'd moved from Vermont a month earlier and were attacked and robbed. The facts in the article didn't quite add up, but these stories were depressing. With no idea of how to earn a living once we got there, Paradise wasn't looking that great.

A day later, I'd reread the article about the Vermont couple three times and my perspective had changed, but still thoughts of the incident lingered. That night I had drinks with some girls from work and I mentioned the article about the new St. Johnians. Being attacked and robbed is a serious thing. Soon, I was relaying all the details outlined in the article.

Once mugged and unconscious, the couple was purported to have been transported, then dumped in the middle of the road next to their house by the robbers. My friends laughed - muggers don't provide taxi service. To have lost all the money they had to their name - four hundred dollars - and a pair of sunglasses worth one hundred and eighty dollars didn't add up, even to me. How could someone have expensive pairs of sunglasses like that if they had so little money to their name? How could they be so dumb as to carry all the money they had in the world with them when they were out drinking? These people admitted they were very drunk and didn't remember much about the night's events. Also they didn't report the crime until six o'clock the next evening. I was laughing with my girlfriends by then at the unlikely tale and it somehow cleansed my mind. All the way home, my thoughts were of the fantasy lives Bob and I would be living in a few short months.

I got home late and Bob was in a down mood. He said he had made little headway on the Internet to prepare for the move. No contacts, no schedule for transporting the car, no job leads. Then he said that after thinking it through we should take only what could fit in our cars to Paradise and store the rest, just in case.

This didn't sound like someone who is looking forward to moving. "Don't you want to move anymore?"

Bob snapped, "Well it looks like crime is real bad". I was stopped cold.

"I'm not staying here," I said, waving my arms to encompass the condo. "Where would we go?"

There was a long silence. And when Bob said "Arizona. Except maybe it gets too hot in the summer. Maybe Alaska."

I had nothing quick to say. My first thought was that his mother's comments and newspaper clippings had gotten the better of him. Then the *Tradewinds* article that I'd discussed only hours ago with friends came rushing back into my consciousness.

"It's the latest issue of the newspaper isn't it?" I asked.

He blurted, "well the panhandling is really bad". I couldn't believe this was the real issue. We'd been through too much in the last few months. I pointed out that panhandling had never been a problem when we visited St. John before. He reminded me we'd been approached in the park on our last visit. Bob was right, but I didn't think it had bothered him. I'd forgotten the incident had happened. It wasn't a fond memory - then again I'd lived in NYC for a while and had become immune. But, there had to be more.

"Wasn't the article about the two people who'd recently moved from New England crazy? That could have been us," he said in a rush.

I laughed and he blinked. Then I had my husband reread the article and shared my newfound perspective. Besides, the incidents reported weren't much if you compared with our own neighborhood. And this was a bi-weekly newspaper. Most of the crimes reported wouldn't have even made our daily paper.

Bob visibly relaxed and admitted, "I guess it's just a little trouble in Paradise".

With less than six months to go we'd both begun feeling insecure. We needed positive reinforcement, but, there was no mention of the incident in *The VI Daily News,* nor was any mention ever made in later *Tradewinds* editions. Weeks passed before the incident faded in our memories and another minor setback in our lives brought a new icon to rejuvenate our spirits towards Paradise.

My automobile's health was in question. I was driving home from work in the dreary dark. The mileage gauge had long ago passed the one-hundred-thousand-mile mark and the car's age was showing. A few weeks ago a dead battery had been replaced and now it needed new tires to get through the coming New England winter. Ten miles into my thirty-seven mile commute on a busy highway, my driver side power window decided it was time to die. In its death throws, the window suddenly powered up without human intervention and literally dropped dead into an open position. It was a record breaking cold rainy day and no amount of coaxing would raise that window.

A visit to a hastily found Ford dealership proved my worst fear had come true. It would cost a minimum of three hundred and fifty dollars to get to the source of the problem and fix it. If there were more wrong than a dead door motor, the cost would go up from there. At home, I layered plastic against the frame and hoped for a sunny week.

The next day was indeed sunny and I was tormented on whether to fix my car or trade it in for something more appropriate to island life. I entered through the passenger side and as I crawled over the center console, I shut the door behind me. The sickening sound of a motor on it's last gasp and the sudden draft at my back ended it. The other window had powered up and dropped open for the last time. The automobile had decided its fate.

A replacement vehicle was already in the budget for the move to St.

John. My little Ford Probe would never survive the steep hills or the dirt roads, even in prime condition. A four-wheel drive vehicle would be much more appropriate to island life. While Bob's four-wheel drive Subaru station wagon was low to the ground, it would be useful for shopping expeditions on St. Thomas. I'd hoped the Probe would survive the winter first, but the cost wasn't worth it.

Unfortunately, there's not a great market for small convertible SUV's like a Samurai or a GEO Tracker in November in New England. But, surprisingly, within a day, I had a new car. The car dealer told us the very pregnant previous owner loved the vehicle. With twins on the way though, she was concerned about the convertible roof and safety for her babies in the back seat. The truth of its history didn't matter. The vehicle was perfect.

It was a fuchsia colored GEO Tracker convertible with a black top and new snow tires and mechanics that were relatively easy to maintain by amateurs. It was hard not to smile and see our future in that pink car. Even Bob got a silly grin on his face whenever he looked at it. Thank goodness the vehicle had a strong heater too. The Tracker was not meant to drive in high winds on busy highways for long distances. But in the winter to come, it would survive and so would we.

Freshly cut pine trees had always had special meaning to me at Christmas time. Every year Bob made a big project of getting together gloves and rope and saws and other trivia and dressing for his annual traipse into the woods, mumbling all the while 'what a good husband' he was. This year was no exception. The first tree we saw, Bob wanted to cut. I just made him hang in there until we passed the third one. It was a major concession on my part. Bob was going through the motions but his heart didn't seem in it. He went holiday shopping with me, but Bob had no holiday spirit. This year he left most of the gift buying and wrapping to me, and all the decorating too. Bob chipped in with some ribbon work and labeling when pushed, but everything was just a chore.

I gave in to the urge to be overly generous to charity this year - maybe I knew it was unlikely we'd be able to afford it in the future. My husband's holiday is Hanukah, but he normally looked forward to getting Christmas gifts as a consolation for putting up with me during the Holidays. To his credit, Bob didn't complain once at the bounty of items that I bought to give to charity. Then again, I'd always looked forward to the arguments over my generosity. His lack of interest in receiving gifts himself was even more disconcerting. So much for traditions.

Many of our Christmas traditions fell by the wayside this year. It was a sad and extremely nostalgic time despite the gayness of the season. In our visits with family, our pending move never came up. I think everyone was feeling the same nostalgia for times past. For the past ten years, Birdie and Dan came to wherever we lived for a little sleep over party just before Christmas. We always ate too much, made silly toasts, and teased each other like twelve-year-olds as only well adjusted adults could. Gifts were exchanged with lots of laughter and love while whacky photographs recorded the whole sordid event. Our best friends fought over the guest bed and the couch for sleeping and we all woke to a long drawn out breakfast before moving on with our lives.

This year, our roles were reversed. The event was held for the first and only time at Birdie's festive condo. We were treated like royalty. Dan's dinner made the last ten we'd cooked seem like mere appetizers. For once Bob and I were mere guests. For the first time since I'd known her, Birdie had a real Christmas tree loaded with ornaments I'd given her over the years. Before desert was served, Bob got caught up in the holiday spirit and began, to our amazement, to hum Christmas carols. Our traditional evening of friendship was followed by an even lazier than normal morning departure - everyone got teary-eyed when Bob and I left.

Some people didn't know what to buy us for the holidays, so they gave us lots of toys for our cats. These two got so many presents, we decided to only let them play with a few. The rest were packed so they'd have new toys in Paradise. Still, Bob received wonderful gifts that we cherished, including water floats and a blender. Bob gave me palm tree shaped wooden ornaments that he'd secretly bought on St. Croix that summer, for our last pine Christmas tree. I guess he'd had the spirit all along.

That New Years Eve was a quietly spent with old neighbors reminiscing about the past and sharing dreams about the future. It had been a fine holiday season... our last in New England. Too soon, it was over.

Chapter Six
Plotting and Planning and Picking and Packing

The New Year brought a renewed sense of commitment and a simple Resolution. Bob and I both vowed to get to Paradise in June while retaining our sanity. It was not a resolution made in jest. While it seemed we'd just finished unpacking, it was time to pack again. We'd become experts at that task. Every item in the garage had been unpacked that fall to make them cockroach-free - even those we'd hoped not to see again until St. John. The garage had only been empty enough for a car for a few weeks but now it would be our staging area. Our sanity was already in doubt.

On a 'warm' Saturday afternoon in January we finally regained some equilibrium. The temperature reached a balmy sixty degrees thanks to the perfect timing of that quirk of nature known locally as the January Thaw. Bob and I donned loose fitting fleece jackets and took our trusty lawn chairs outside to the small deck attached to the condo.

DESIRING PARADISE

He tempted the fates with his shorts while I remained snug in a pair of old sweatpants. Within minutes we were both content, soaking up the winter sun. It was a perfect time to philosophize and share ideas.

We contemplated the months ahead of us. Before we decided what and how to repack, we had to decide how we would move our possessions. Bob told me this plotting and planning was like preparing for a long canoe expedition. He'd just finished reading a travel essay about a couple that'd canoed across Canada for a solid year.

"Preparation was the key to their survival," he said.

"These folks had prepared to have major supplies waiting for them at the canoe put-in site, and then supplies timed to be air dropped to remote villages they would pass on the way. They would get the supplies they needed when they needed them and not a moment before." I caught his excitement as he continued.

"When they started their expedition, they brought just what they would need to get to the first drop-off point. Everything they brought was a necessity that had multiple uses like we're doing."

Bob rarely talked so much in a single day, so I prodded him on. Our own trip would be different yet we could use some of the same concepts. He'd obviously given our own expedition a great deal of thought. His monologue continued with ideas on the logistics.

"Our automobiles have to be driven to Florida. As for the rest of our things, options range from hiring an expensive global shipping company, to hauling our goods ourselves to Florida, the closest point on the continent to the USVI. This last option means hiring a consolidator for shipment to St. Thomas and then a hiring a truck to barge it all to St. John. Or, we could mail everything to ourselves via the US Post Office."

This last option tickled my senses as I tried to stifle a giggle.

"Mailing your life's possessions is considered a practical way to move by most St. Johnians," Bob insisted. No kidding. Maybe it was the warm sun in the middle of the winter. But his idea made sense to me. It fit with his concept of this move as a 'life expedition' and seemed doable since we wouldn't be taking much furniture.

Using the motto 'If It Can't Be Mailed, It Can't Be Needed' we shook hands in the waning sunlight and sealed the plan to somehow mail our life to Paradise.

With our expedition, nothing could be left behind. One person would need to go ahead of the other to secure lodging and a mailing address. That pioneer would take some things, with the rest of our goods to follow. The other person would wrap up our life in New England and ship boxes for immediate needs. Friends and neighbors would ship any remaining boxes over time. There was no mention of who would go first and who would come later. We both envisioned ourselves as that first pioneer.

Since we'd be relying on the US Post Office as our lifeline getting a Post Office box was crucial. We'd been told there was a two-hundred person waiting list, which turned out to be true. We'd filled out the request form for our own months ago but were way down on the list. So why didn't we just ship everything ahead of time in care of General Delivery to the on-island Post Office? Our sanity was in question, but we were not crazy.

We planned to have most boxes timed to arrive exactly when we needed them and not a moment before. It meant depending on friends and old neighbors to help us out, but we were confident they could be counted on. Even those who were still in denial over our plans would probably help out. Christmas boxes wouldn't be needed in July, but we'd be homesick for maple syrup by August. If we could figure out the Post Office timing, it could work. We hadn't quite ironed out the specifics, but it made sense.

The next day, the remaining skeleton of our Christmas tree came down and we began the work we'd be doing every week for the next twenty weeks...packing. Sanity became an increasingly elusive goal. I used cloth decorations and garland to line the outer sides of those first Christmas cartons. A couple of kitty toys were included as a holiday surprise for the cats, and videos on skiing and winter kayaking for Bob. I included anything I could think of that we would only use during the holiday season. This whole timing approach was kind of fun... at the beginning.

As I packed, I was again whittling down the things we'd take. It was very hard to throw out anything - even ornaments that were ratty looking after years of abuse. Though I threw out more than I packed, habit made me shop after Christmas sales to buy new mini-lights, wrapping paper, and tags. At the discount I got they were worth the price to buy, pack, and ship. We had a cheap plastic Christmas tree stand we'd bought to replace the great iron one someone inadvertently sold at our last yard sale in the fall. I insisted it was a multi-use item that would be of great value on the island, although I had no idea what else it could be used for. Bob just shook his head and wisely let it be packed.

The plan for our vehicles to find their way to Paradise came naturally. Our new St. Croix friends had discussed freely with us the pros and cons of buying vehicles locally versus barging them over from the mainland. We knew what we had to do. Each of us would drive an automobile to Florida, where we'd put our cars on barges and then fly to St. Thomas, with our autos arriving hopefully a few days later. Both vehicles would be going - mine because the GEO Tracker was bought for this purpose and his because it was paid for and it could carry lots of things. We had the 'beauty' and the 'beast'. Our vehicles were known assets to this expedition and the price to ship them was relatively small.

We'd been cautioned to find a barge that would travel directly from the mainland to St. Thomas, without stopping first in Puerto Rico. This would minimize the likelihood that our vehicles would arrive missing a headlight or battery or other key component. A good friend in San Juan confirmed this. "It's sad, but sometimes I think ripping people off is a national pastime here," he said. I didn't know if I believed it or if he was just paranoid. Soon it was a mute point. Bob found a shipping company that would barge the cars directly to St. Thomas. They promised it would take only take three to four days for the vehicles to make their ocean trip.

The cats would be a problem. We couldn't leave them behind because they were like our children. Both had adapted quickly to their three story luxuriously carpeted condo from their long 'vacation' with Birdie up north. Our outdoor adventurer and our indoors-bred princess had been limited to indoors for the duration. Their months together were wearing thin and our outdoor adventurer showed signs of cabin fever. We attempted a compromise. My husband came home one Saturday with gifts for our feline pets. A blue walking harness for him and a more petite pink one for the princess. Both cats were offended. The adventurer eventually came around, and accepted the harness with resignation. But, no matter how often we tried, after a short few minutes outdoors, our outdoor guy demanded his freedom. We were afraid he would hurt himself or get loose, so we had to permanently curtail his efforts.

Our feline princess wanted nothing to do with the outdoors. She'd be living partially outdoors on St. John and we wanted her to get used to it. After weeks spent to get her out of hiding just to get her to accept the harness, she was ready. Her Royal Highness had a great paranoia of large spaces. Whenever we took her outside, she'd drop onto her belly and crawl fast in a beeline fashion back to the outside door. She'd never lasted past ten seconds of petting to soothe her before she'd claw her way into that belly crawl no matter what the weather or location. The harness made no difference. Within two seconds of being placed on the ground, that cat was out of her harness and doing the fast belly crawl.

Perhaps it wasn't worth the effort. Our princess would never go off and get lost like our outdoor adventurer would likely do within days on-island. We just hoped the little gal be happy living in a place where outdoors and indoors were often separated only by some invisible line.

I thought the cats could be flown down as 'cargo' from New England on an airplane, but that wouldn't work. According to the airlines, the timing of flights and connections meant the cats couldn't get there to arrive when Customs was still open for the day in Miami or San Juan. Someone would have to meet their flight at the connecting location, take the cats overnight and return them to Customs the next day. Then they could continue their journey to St. Thomas. One of us would have to pick them up at the airport and ferry them to St. John. There had to be a better way.

I created an inventory on my computer of all the things we were packing. For lack of something better, it was titled the *Paradise Expedition*. Bob was inspired enough to tack the topographical maps of St. John and St. Thomas onto our living room wall. He also put up a road map of St. John for further reference. The maps would be studied often and reminded us to focus every time we passed through the room.

Checking reference points on the maps, we were able to locate neighborhood names we read about in the newspapers. We learned a lot. First there were the high crime areas. We wouldn't want to live there. Then came the most desirable living areas, which we determined from the most expensive real estate ads. We'd want to live close by. A serious flaw in this logic became apparent immediately. These neighborhoods were one and the same. High property values meant temptation to some. We revised the plan to look for long term rentals in neighborhoods that were rarely mentioned in the news. Our friends laughed, but it worked.

In line with our packing scheme, each box was identified by the month targeted for arrival, along with a separate box identifier. Boxes 11-1 and 11-2 would hopefully arrive by November, if all went perfectly. If it worked, the unpacking and storage process at the other end of the world would be simple if drawn out. Packed boxes were growing along every wall in the condo. I tired not to think about slow unpacking at the other end of our move. Bob re-read his many books on expedition travel looking for clues on what and how to pack and often gave me advice that contradicted packing I'd just completed. I stifled the urge to kill him when he insisted that these books be taken with us, as they'd be 'invaluable for the rest of our lives'.

Because things do get 'lost' in the mail, we couldn't send all the linens in a single box although packing it that way would have been simpler. Consolidating into one box would tempt the fates. I had visions of checking the post office every day until I couldn't take sleeping any longer without my 'things'. I'd finally break down and we'd buy all new linens on St. John for some astronomical price. The box would, of course, arrive the next day. And so, the linens went into three separate boxes.

Bob's research dictated that every box should be tightly packed, so jarring would cause no movement. As long as a box was well padded and packed so that nothing could move, nothing would break. Towels, pillows rolls of toilet paper and paper towels were used along with more traditional bubble wrap and peanut shaped packing materials for cushioning. There were an unbelievable number of small items that could fill every nook and cranny of each box we packed. Scissors, flashlights, Band-Aids, pens, notepads and a myriad of other items we had in multiple supply were split up and shipped as filler items across multiple boxes.

I discovered that scissors could be stuffed inside the cardboard that held wrapping paper, and that the insides of a coffeepot could handle lots of extra things. Sometimes a few luxury items were packed - maple syrup packed in four different boxes, and brownie and chili mixes to ease adjustment of our taste buds to local fare. We overdid it. I forgot the world now lives in a global economy. When I couldn't lift a box after two hours packing tightly, I remembered an important factor. Box weight was an issue. The television was packed without my help. Bob didn't want to hear my grief. We were out of control.

The *Paradise Expedition* had meanwhile evolved from a simple inventory to a complete shipping manual. A Table of Contents listed a summary of the contents of each box. Each box had it's own page in the manual with a detailed inventory and the rough box weight found by using our trusty bathroom scale. The Post Office proved our scale was accurate to the pound. The scale, we left behind. The *Paradise Expedition* concluded with an index showing each item cross-referenced. Now I could see that the boxes on page 3, 9, and 30 all had pool-toys, while boxes on page 5, 14, and 26 contained aspirin.

While we weren't moving for five months, I felt the time was right to inform my employer formally of my intentions. It was a big step. But it would take time to hire or promote a replacement and I had a small staff who deserved to be told so I verbally resigned my position as of the end of May. Management was supportive and more surprised than they should have been. I'd been telling them for two years of my plan to move to Paradise and, when asked, of our progress. Some of these folks would end up mailing us boxes.

At work a few weeks later, I had a meeting that included my vice president. It was to be prophetic. I hadn't spoken to him since the conference call when I'd announced my last day. At the beginning of the meeting, he shook my hand in greeting.

"Thanks for deciding to stay," he joked.

"And thank you for having the foresight and willingness to let me Tele-commute from my new home," I quipped without thinking. We both blinked and then smiled as the seeds of possibility grew in both of our heads at the same time.

Perhaps the job advice Bob and I had consistently gotten from local USVI residents during our vacations wouldn't be needed. We'd been told to plan on each person having three jobs. One for the healthcare benefits, one to pay some bills, and one to have some fun while making some money. The trick we were told is to link various skills and hobbies together to eke out a reasonable living. It was hard to imagine. I hadn't been able to picture just one thing Bob or I could each do for a living, much less six jobs total.

After a few weeks of our expedition-planning phase we were really getting into the rhythm. Though we were waist high in boxes and packing, putting the maps up had made a psychological difference. Most boxes were packed in the living room, with the wall maps quietly coaching. Yes, I talked to them when things got tough. My cats gave me strange looks. Holiday gifts were often packed in their unopened wrappers - water floats, baking utensils, towels and so on. Our new blender was saved this fate and was nearly the last item we packed. We experimented with exotic drink preparation to perk us up on especially dreary winter weekends. In six weeks twenty-seven boxes had been packed, marked with the intended delivery month and inventoried and stored in the garage. Double those amounts of things were just waiting to be packed. Packing was getting out of hand.

It took creativity to get some 'difficult' items packed. An old ski bag took care of a kayak paddle, 6 tiki lamps, some table legs, and a large roll of unprimed artist's canvas. This last item had traveled through ten years of our relationship - from apartment, to house, to condo - and I swear I'd never seen it before. Bob's favorite paddle wasn't worth the effort to complain about, and the tiki lamps were a matter of principle for both of us. One of us would take the ski bag to Florida, check it as luggage for the plane trip to St. Thomas and pray the airport taxi drivers on-island wouldn't think we were loco.

That February we celebrated our wedding anniversary in Stowe, Vermont staying in the same suite at the inn where we'd honeymooned nine years earlier. For months we'd debated whether we should spend the seemingly extravagant amount of money it cost for this little vacation, but in the end we decided life was too short and deserved to be enjoyed once in a while. The wonderful inn was owned and operated by a transplanted British couple who believed strongly in personalized service and who paid close attention to the little details that made fond vacation memories. As a result of our numerous past visits, our names were forever enshrined on a small brass plaque in their adjoining pub. We wanted to say good-bye.

It was a delightful and nostalgic time. Doubtful we'd be back any-time soon, we took full advantage of our few days there. The family budget was stretched for cross country skiing, skating, shopping, and even a movie at the local theatre. Every afternoon we enjoyed after-noon tea and delicate pastries in front of a roaring fire. Bob loved his daily bubble bath in our private Jacuzzi with a half-pint of imported draft ale by his side. I loved the Laura Ashley bedroom with all its frills and colors. Our yearly visits to the Cranford Suite were a luxury we'd be leaving behind, so we cherished these things more dearly than ever before.

On the day after Valentine's day and upon our return home, Bob and I fought over who would get to be the first pioneer to Paradise. I lost. Forging the trail ahead had probably always been Bob's aspiration. The first time I met my husband-to-be was at a health club where he told me his name was "Ranger Bob". For the next six months, that was the only name I knew him by as he strutted through the club gaining the confidence to ask me out on a date. Since then my life had become one big uncharted adventure.

Despite and perhaps because of the cockroach incident, Bob insisted on a chance to redeem himself by proving his home-hunting capa-bilities were real. Willingness to handle necessary but mundane tasks like setting up bank accounts, getting utilities hooked up, and fighting for a post office box was indisputable. Bob would drive his box filled car to Florida alone and document the trip. My travel a few weeks later was to be a simple matter of following his path. With two cats fighting for their freedom all the way. In a Geo Tracker convertible. Oh, yes... I lost.

A single phone call the next day put me in much better spirits.

"Hello, I'd like to book a one-way ticket for my husband to leave the country. Can you help me?" I queried the airline representative on the phone.

"Lady, I've waited my whole career for someone to say that!" chuckled the agent.

And to think, I'd only been waiting years. Never mind that I felt compelled to explain I'd be following my husband a few weeks later. It made for great office cooler chitchat that day. Bob now had firm travel plans to Paradise with ninety days to spare before the great expedition began.

It seemed right to begin the countdown. A calendar was marked up with all of Bob's key dates - when to give notice at work, when to leave town, when to have the car to the dock in Florida, when to take his final flight. It was scary not having a home already for him in St. John but I was beginning to have faith that it would all fall into place. For him. None of my dates were firm yet.

I couldn't believe how nice the folks at work were being. Their support made me work extra hard to make sure the move didn't interfere with my workload. One clue this strategy was paying off came in a form I wasn't expecting. An industry-wide convention was to be held in Las Vegas in May. The week long event is always hard work but lots of fun too. While my staff needed to attend, I anticipated that I would be absent this year. Over eighty thousand people would attend the event and hotel rooms and airline tickets had to be secured early so I sent in the company-required approval forms for my staff, but left myself off the list. My boss noticed.

To my surprise, he stopped me in the hall one day and insisted that 'of course' I'd be going. I felt humbled and yet proud - and promised myself I'd do a good job. It would give me a last chance to say good-bye to many cross-country business acquaintances while being productive to my organization right up to the end. The month of May would be very eventful.

Unfortunately, Bob didn't have the same workplace support. His company was young, known to escort people immediately out the door upon their resignation. This made it much more risky for Bob to discuss our pending move, get feedback and make plans to leave his job gracefully. He would simply give a two-week notice and hope for the best when the time came. Only a few close work-mates knew of his plans. Meanwhile, Bob was searching *The VI Daily News* for job opportunities.

A casual discussion at my workplace developed into a possible employment opportunity for Bob. I met a business associate who was a sales representative for another company. He told me his territory included the Caribbean and Latin America. When I told him that Bob and I were moving to St. John, he surprised me by telling me one of his distributors was Bestech, the only small computer business on St. John. I shared that Bob had visited their office on our last vacation, and was preparing to write to them in search of a job.

The Latin America businessman shocked me with firsthand news that indeed the owner had been considering hiring some additional help. While he wasn't quite ready to do so, the owner had plans to hire someone in the next few months. They'd been discussing the difficulty in finding good help only two weeks earlier during a business trip to St. John. It was perfect. This wonderful man, on his own, went one step further and put in a good word for Bob with Bestech. It was an unasked for kindness we would never forget.

Afraid to hope, Bob quickly sent off his letter of inquiry to St. John. From that moment on, he was focused and determined to land a job in Paradise before he arrived. Newspapers, the Internet, and even the library were consulted on a regular basis. On a practical note, if one of us could find a job similar to our present ones before we moved, then the move might qualify as a tax deduction. My retired accountant father was proud of us.

Our financial position was a constant concern. I wavered between feeling okay with our budget and being paranoid that it wasn't enough. We'd collected both depressing and uplifting books on the subject. When I got paranoid, I'd pull out the one titled "How to Live Without a Salary" and remind myself that we were doing our best to cover all the bases. If anything, according to the book, we were overly concerned.

So far, I'd had to increase our estimate for our first year's living expenses three separate times. The surprising thing was that we'd been able to escalate our savings to compensate, despite our occasional extravagances. As time went along, we managed to improve on our savings almost every month. We were hoping to have steady incomes despite the book's comments that we could find ways to survive without them. And we were determined to be prepared for anything.

A packing consideration was the price of shipping versus the value of the items to be shipped. This guessing game added an extra challenge to our packing strategy. St. John is a small island with limited shopping for everyday items and we'd never tried to buy household items or small appliances in the US Virgin Islands. There are major department stores on St. Thomas and we expected to pay more for non-sale items. But how much more was a pure guess. Some items we packed and shipped were a big mistake. We have four huge boxes of miscellaneous computer parts growing more obsolete with every day which can attest to that fact.

"Metal will rust. Plastic is also lighter to pack." This piece of husbandly wisdom came long after the metal mixing bowls and utensils were already packed, sealed and indexed. But, it gave me an idea. There would be a need to store things on St. John. Cardboard boxes were a favorite breeding ground for cockroaches. Also, they weren't waterproof which could be a problem in the hurricane prone Caribbean. If we could ship items in plastic boxes, we could recycle them for storage bins. I checked with the US Post Office and discovered there was no restriction, provided the boxes weren't breakable. My husband can be so smart at times.

As time for the move grew closer, even those friends who'd thought we were crazy offered to help. Their change of heart was graciously accepted. We needed thirty people to ship us two or three boxes each over time. Logistics were tricky, as some willing people couldn't store boxes for long. Others could store boxes, but had back problems so they couldn't help with any box of significant weight. Some could store items for only a month or two. It was like a puzzle. Small people would get small boxes and strong ones the heavier boxes. Weird friends got weird boxes. Matching people to boxes, weights and delivery dates took real skill. If only there were a job on St. John for this kind of thing, Bob and I would be all set.

Out of the first sixteen people we asked to store and/or mail boxes, only one person said "no". Most people were willing to handle more than we asked for. We tried hard not to take advantage of their generous offers. After a couple of trips to the Post Office, I was sure they'd regret their exuberance.

Already two people had asked to schedule their vacations to visit us - one in October and one for the Christmas holiday. I hoped many would come to visit - it would be nice. It would have been nicer if we had a clue where we'd be living or if we'd be working. But 'visitors' made it sound like we were already local residents and the fantasy brought warm feelings.

Two days earlier the outside temperature had hit an unseasonable seventy degrees. That night, a major snowstorm hit the region with over two feet of snow by dawn. Bob's company announced on the radio early in the morning that his workplace was closed for the day.

Since my company rarely closed its doors, I'd hoped to work remotely and avoid the thirty-seven mile commute through the snow, but I couldn't get through on my computer. Bummer.

Moments later, Bob called me excitedly from the living room. A miracle had occurred. My workplace too had decided to close shop due to the storm. I thought he was mistaken, but then the radio interrupted its broadcast for a news flash from the State Governor. He declared a 'state of emergency', called up the National Guard to assist in clearing the roads and urged everyone to stay home and off the roads for the day. There would definitely be no work for either of us that day. Then we lost power.

We had no driveway to shovel and we had no work commitments. Losing power was a minor problem. It gave us a chance to play with our hurricane preparedness skills. We located the candles and the flashlights and the propane stove. Since it was daylight, we didn't need even these things. But, Bob made a huge breakfast on our temporary stove just for fun and we plotted our day of freedom. We vowed to do no packing or anything else resembling responsible adult activities. It was nearly the end of winter and we were being given a gift of some magical time together.

By late morning, the storm itself had passed and the sun was shining brightly. It was a day for childish laughter and fun I never thought I'd experience again. Out came the cross-country skis and the last of the hot chocolate. A little cruise through the neighborhood on skis, snow angels in the parking lot, and photographs of the snow-laden trees to keep the memory alive. Soon a few snowballs were exchanged. My aim was just not as good as my husbands. I ducked behind my Geo Tracker. It was parked outside, having lost the nightly race home to be the first vehicle into the garage. Behind this sturdy fortress I could avoid most of my husbands rapid-fire snowballs. I was laughing so hard I had tears in my eyes, as I continued to throw snowy projectiles as fast as I could.

There was a sudden lull in the action. I peeked over the hood of the car, only to find Bob ready with a snowball in each fist. He was laughing so hard his aim was bad. Slam - they both landed squarely on the hood of the car, as I ducked around the front.

I swear the headlights on my Tracker winked and the front grill widened into a grin for just a split second. My vision was blurred, but I know what I saw. Stunned, I called a truce. It was a magical time and the last snow day we'd ever live through. Life was good.

St. John Trivia

The highest point on St. John is Bordeaux Mountain, with a peak that's 1277 feet above sea level. Folks living in the Bordeaux area generally report temperature readings that are 5 - 8 degrees lower than those reported in Cruz Bay. In contrast, the salt pond between Salt Pond Bay and Trunk Bay is one foot below sea level while the trench in the ocean between St. John and St. Croix is more than 12,000 feet deep.

In 1998 a rare event occurred on St. John . . . a hailstorm. Despite the calm sunny day, the hail fell for fifteen minutes on the Ram's Head Trail. Tourists, returning from Ram's Head Point, the southernmost point on St. John, were caught in the sudden barrage. It hails on St. John about once every hundred years.

Chapter Seven
The Countdown

My husband's expedition timeline was posted in the kitchen for all to see. His excitement over his pending travel through Americana grew daily until it became unbearable. I couldn't help being jealous. I would be the 'cleanup' person staying behind and though it was only for six weeks, it loomed like a lifetime. Our on-paper savings were down - the whole stock market was down - and the timing was bad to liquidate some investments for our first year's funds. Bob was supportive of my decisions, leaving the finances up to me. I was on the fourth notebook of re-working the numbers and felt burdened but couldn't complain. After all, he trusted me.

"Why couldn't we be the type of people that need nothing more than a change of clothes and a toothbrush to keep us happy?" I lamented one night. Sixty-five boxes of goods and books were catalogued, assigned to 'designated mailers' and cross-referenced in The *Paradise*

Expedition manual. Ten more boxes were in process. Our condo was an obstacle course. We had to start delivering boxes to friends for storage, just to make space to walk.

Bob found a classified ad in *The VI Daily News* for a job that mirrored his resume - he responded in writing within an hour of reading the details. It was much more promising than most 'feelers' he'd been sending out. Bestech, known as "The Computer Guys" on St. John was still a possibility as he'd been exchanging letters and phone calls with Chuck, the manager, but nothing concrete had developed. I guessed this kind of initiative was what it would take to find jobs. But I stalled doing the same, even when I saw job ads appropriate for my skills. My company had been hinting about having me continue working in some capacity such as a contractor or even as a part-time employee. It wasn't something I should have counted on, but I did.

Minor medical problems plagued us. In March, I had a dental emergency while traveling on business. Halfway between Boston and San Antonio, Texas, I began to have serious tooth pain. I knew the signs too well - I needed a root canal. When we landed, my first phone call was to my dentist, who'd spent years rectifying the damage caused by poor childhood dental work. During the course of multiple bridges, capped teeth and multiple root canals, we'd developed a strong working relationship. Living fifty miles away hadn't changed my opinion. He was the best.

My call to his office brought my dentist chuckling to the phone. He immediately asked "are you in the Virgin Islands?" He was disappointed we hadn't moved yet, but not surprised I was traveling on business. My dentist had become used to the occasional travel emergency from his favorite patient. Without hesitation, he phoned in a prescription to a nationwide drugstore chain. By the time my business meeting started in the morning, I was on antibiotics and hopeful.

My business took me onward that day to California. Despite the pills, my pain was getting worse with each mile. A very important business dinner with a vendor was scheduled that evening. The restaurant was a five-star Epicurean delight, but even a sip of tepid water made me cry out in pain. Luckily, my dinner partner was late. Chewing was not a viable option but I was hungry. I shyly explained my problem to the hovering waiter, who agreed to see what the chef could do to adapt the menu for me. My business associate raised a quick eyebrow when I told him I'd pre-ordered my meal, but kept his thoughts to himself. Every spoonful brought tears of pain as I nibbled on pureed potatoes and squash and poached salmon, but the negotiations went on as planned. I was difficult to please that night.

Sleep wasn't a consideration in my hotel room hours later. I couldn't take the pain anymore. The medication was not working. An urgent message to my dentists' answering service brought a quickly returned phone call, a confirmed diagnosis and a new prescription at a nearby pharmacy. He assured me I'd feel better by morning and asked me to call him with an update the next afternoon. At the designated time, my dentist said he'd located a colleague nearby in California who was willing to see me first thing the next morning. But, my pain was now bearable and I was determined to fly home on schedule at daybreak, so he insisted I call him when I landed in Boston. Before the weekend was over, so was the crisis. Another root canal completed.

Two days later, Bob's podiatrist confirmed he had tendonitis between the first and second toe on his right foot. Another week, another medical problem. His injury was the result of pushing too hard against the foot pegs in his kayak and brought Bob six weeks of physical therapy. Determined to stop this recurring injury, Bob got a friend to replace the foot pegs with a foam bulkhead he created just for the boat... the boat that would stay behind in New England. I was sure Bob's problem was history.

My husband attempted to fly to Rochester, New York, to visit his mother. Unlike me, he rarely traveled by airplane. It was to be his good-bye visit and he wanted to go alone. While the weather was fine when Bob left the condo, by the time he reached the airport it had changed. His flight got canceled due to weather, as was the next flight. All the other flights for the weekend were overbooked. Bob persevered at the airport, waiting on the standby list for later flights, but after eight hours at the Boston airport he realized the situation was hopeless. Without a backup plan, and with time running out, it would be difficult reschedule this important trip.

We learned. Contingency plans were drawn up for every aspect of our move. We coordinated our calendars for the next sixty days and added in some 'reserved' days to handle future catastrophes. It wasn't until Mothers Day that my husband managed to squeeze in a short but worthwhile visit to his mom. We both scheduled full physical exams and preventative health visits to slow down the inevitable health problems. Our schedules were getting overloaded.

A death in the family brought home our own mortality. While my aunt had been ailing for a long time, as always death came unexpectedly. Our family had never been a close one and it always took a major life event to bring us together. Assisting as a pallbearer, my husband discovered our distant family members didn't know we were planning to move. With our parents only slightly younger than my aunt who had just died, some disapproved of our plans. It was an uncomfortable situation.

April came and with it went our US Federal Tax returns and lots of cash to pay for our investment sins. Next year, our Federal taxes would be paid to and refunds paid by the VI Internal Revenue Bureau. Meanwhile, all the newspapers from the USVI confirmed a fact that we had believed to be idle rumor. Many people hadn't received their refund checks yet for prior tax years. For up to three years earlier. It was strongly advised that VI residents should endeavor to owe moneys at the end of the year. It was not a pleasant thought.

One night in late April, I had dinner with a friend and she marveled that we could make this big change in our lives without any hesitation. Hesitations? The urge to push out the actual move date was sometimes strong. Bob was scheduled to leave town in a month, but we didn't have a place to live, firm job prospects or a support system on St. John to take the edge off. We were handing out our personal possessions to people without a guarantee we would ever see them again - and we didn't even have an address where they'd be mailed.

With time running out, we moved into high gear. About fifteen boxes had already been delivered to people who would later mail them to us. I promised to deliver instructions and money for shipping costs once we figured it all out. There were still empty boxes in every room in the condo waiting to be packed and items I didn't know we owned started appearing like magic next to those boxes. My darling husband suddenly 'found' over fifty T-shirts that he couldn't live without. He had hidden them until the last moment in hopes I wouldn't throw them away. Having packed craft items that I might never make anything with, I begrudgingly gave in and counted the days until Bob left town.

The Spring West River Weekend was upon us. It would be the end of the tradition, and we were nostalgic about the event. I enjoyed telling everyone at work that I was heading to Jamaica for a long weekend at the end of a dark cold winter. "But we don't have to drive through Peru to get there... Peru Vermont, that is. That's ten miles *north* of Jamaica." I babbled. We needed a weekend away.

Our friend, Dan, was in love and brought his new girlfriend camping for the first time this spring. I knew she was a 'keeper' when she shared her long held secret desire to visit St. John someday. It was also a secret dream of Dan's. But first they had to survive the weekend. As usual, the campground was littered with mounds of snow and pools of ice over eight inches thick where constant freezing and thawing had left its mark. The days warmed up but the nights were downright cold. While the kayakers did their thing, the rest of us took day trips around the countryside.

Birdie joined us as usual and looked forward to at least one quality girl's day out. As we warmed our toes in the car and headed out of the campground we decided to play 'the driving game' one last time to make exploring the back roads of Vermont more challenging. That weekend we decided that we could only travel in a straight line or take left turns. Right turns were not permitted. Even a 'straight right' such as a right-side fork in a road when the steering wheel needn't turn was unacceptable. The goal was to avoid repeating any road and yet to return to the campsite no earlier than sunset. No maps were allowed.

We covered almost every dirt road in south/central Vermont that day, talking about the past and of the future the whole way. Birdie would be traveling with me all the way to St. John as both a companion and an assistant to help with the cats. She had lots of ideas on how we might while away the long days driving to Florida. Some made me laugh and some made me cringe, but all made me sure we'd have an adventuresome trip together. Almost before we blinked, it was late afternoon and we were only three left turns and thirty miles away from the campground.

Birdie and I usually prepared the bulk of the traditional Saturday evening feast. But this time, another campsite friend smoked a turkey and other guests prepared all the fixings for a Thanksgiving-like feast. Someone had brought a portable boom box and continually played a tape of bird sounds throughout the evening. One kayaker kept calling off the names of the birds and was amazed they were awake and chirping so late into the night. No one told him he was listening to a tape recording or that he got all the birds names wrong. We didn't want to ruin his fun.

The next morning Bob's knees were killing him from climbing over the dam the day before to get his kayak to the put-in site. The king of omelet making in our group prepared our traditional Sunday breakfast, while friends stopped by the campsite and offered to buy Bob's whitewater kayak since he wouldn't be using it in the islands. Each offer seemed to depress him more. Bob wouldn't budge. He was determined to store it somewhere in New England until he could come back and paddle on some future vacation. Before the day was out, we'd given away excess camping gear to everyone who stopped by. Bob took hundreds of photos that day instead of kayaking. It was the end of an era.

Back home, each delivery of boxes meant a social visit also filled with nostalgia and dreams for the future. Often we shared a beer or snack and stayed far too long. We were saying our pre-farewells to everyone one by one. Sleep was elusive.

In early May, my Las Vegas convention meant a week away from packing. For the first time in four years, Bob stayed behind. Because he'd be giving notice at his place of work the week before the event, he didn't ask his company to send him too. All week, as I met with business associates I attempted to establish continuity for my staff who would carry on after I was gone. I had little time for sleep and called home only twice. Unsolved expedition details haunted my husband, and I realized being remote brought some advantages.

Ever since Bob learned that his company's policy was to show people the front door when they quit, he'd hoped that would happen to him so he could have two extra weeks of free time before his move. Since Bob was responsible for maintaining the company's phones, voice-mail, PC's, networks and so on, sanity prevailed and his hopes were dashed. While I was in Las Vegas, he was working long hours despite handing in his resignation. His workmates thought he was a lucky guy. They even threw him a going away party. Meanwhile Bob was still pursuing job opportunities, and while under consideration for a couple of jobs, nothing was firm.

I started a list of items Bob would need to purchase on St. Thomas once he had a place for us to live. Heavy items that needed replacing like frying pans and fragile ones like everyday drinking glasses could be bought on St. Thomas for prices comparable to here - when on sale. The final phase of expedition planning was upon us.

Maintaining a good work attitude took effort but continued to pay off for me. Talks continued about keeping me as an employee. A telephone company was running a series of TV commercials focusing on 'telecommuters' - people working from home or the beach while performing typical high-tech white-collar jobs. It seemed that everyone we knew had watched these commercials and assumed they depicted my future Tele-commuting life-style. They depicted a glamorous life-style but I suspected the reality might be much different. Even working part-time for my company, I envisioned regular long business trips, first by car, then by ferry, and then by a taxi van - all just to get to the airport and the start of any business trip. I worried that these commercials would negatively impact my company's decision for my future.

I often found myself holding my breath with the uncertainty we faced. Almost every moment was stressful. It didn't help with people coming up to me at work asking if I was ready to move, or if I was counting down the days - that just made me more nervous. Having a place to live, jobs, local bank accounts, insurance, or even a clue would make life easier. Our faith in the future would have impressed a nineteen-year-old as long as they didn't know the truth of our fears.

Bob's thoughts were consumed with his trip to Florida, the process of delivering his car to the barge and boxes to the shipping company and every petty detail in between. I was beginning to realize there was a big advantage in traveling a month later than Bob. The benefit of Bob's experiences would simplify my own trip. It would help out a lot since traveling with the cats meant lots of stress for everyone in the car.

We secured an Internet address as of June 1st with a local service provider in the USVI. This was a major accomplishment, as communicating with others via e-mail would surely cut down on our phone bill costs, even with the added monthly costs to an Internet Service Provider for e-mail access. Bob planned to take his computer to Florida and then mail it so it would be at the Post Office when he arrived on island. Constant communication would be ours. We started to give out our address to technically inclined friends immediately, which eased our minds if nothing else.

We pre-packed Bob's car with boxes earmarked for the trip. Our friends laughed at this, saying we'd taken the planning to the ridiculous. It was a good thing we did it. The car couldn't handle the number of boxes we'd thought. Bob packed all his clothes into a big canvas bag planned as one piece of his airline luggage allowance. But, even his arms strengthened by years of kayaking couldn't lift the overflowing bag more than a few inches off the ground. The whole luggage plan needed rethinking.

My own pre-moving checklist was growing. I had to close our bank accounts and utilities, have our mail forwarded, pay the bills, throw out what we weren't shipping and get the cat vaccinations and health certificates. Then I had to prep for my own trip to Florida with the cats, survive my last days of work, say my last good-byes and figure out whatever we'd forgotten. It seemed like this move would never end.

I found a St. John's bulletin board on the Internet and left a message to the world saying we were moving and desperate and asking for opinions and advice. Amazing - within the first twenty-four hours we heard from someone in Arizona of all places who has lived on St. John off and on most of his life. He had great advice and even a lead on an apartment. The apartment didn't pan out, his insights on a St. John long-term rental agency did. The e-mail marked the point our luck started to change.

Within days we'd sent off a check to the long-term rental agency with our deposit for a two-bedroom apartment. No longer did we consider it crazy to rent sight unseen. The only downside was that we couldn't secure a lease. The search had uncovered only one viable apartment, but the owner wanted the option of moving in himself for the months of December and January. Still, it was workable. He was willing to let us rent on a month to month basis, which would buy us time to find another place for the long term, without concern about an initial place to live. We felt pretty confident about finding an alternative abode by then.

Bob decided not to wait to start a 'business' in the USVI. We chose the name Paradise Expeditions, to give the business 'substance'. It was a prudent decision. Apparently, as a business, we would get a Post Office Box much quicker than as a residential customer would. The waiting list for a residential Post Office Box was still long. We might be on that list forever. So what if our business was undefined?

"The Computer Guys" on St. John told Bob they would put him to work immediately upon his arrival. He was psyched. How it would all work he didn't know and was afraid to ask. It was employment of some sort and that's all that mattered. My employer confirmed I'd be working at least part time for my company, in 'some' capacity. I kept my fingers crossed that I could do so as an employee rather than a contractor, but I too didn't push the issue. My company did not have telecommuters yet that I knew of except in Field Sales positions, but I hoped they would let me be an experiment for future work trends. Bob and I were excited that our dreams were becoming reality and didn't care what form they took.

Plans called for Bob to drive directly to Florida without delay, driving eight to ten hours per day, with a day to rest once the car and its contents were safely on the barge to the USVI. The extra day would suffice for any travel emergencies along the way or in Florida. Our shipping company was located in an unsafe area in southern Florida according to two local taxi companies. Neither would agree to pick Bob up from the shipping office to drive him to a car rental office. Finally, he found a car rental company that would meet him at the barge office and drive him to their rental office to do paperwork and get temporary wheels.

Though major concerns were suddenly coming together better than we'd hoped, we were expecting the inevitable disaster. What if one of the cars had a major catastrophe on its way south? What if one of our pets got sick or lost? What if we lost our luggage or cash? As our plans solidified before our eyes, our imaginations compensated with unknown disasters lurking in the future. Our friends were convinced by this time that we were risk takers - if only they knew. Caution was our middle name.

Bob got multiple notarized copies of our car titles - we'd been told we'd need them to get our cars on island, get insurance and get them registered. That old faded USVI license plate on my office wall had kept me focused and motivated in moments of doubt for the past two years. It was a symbol of our dream. At my own going away party held by my office, I bequeathed that license plate to someone who had his own dream, as a good-luck charm.

My friends gave me a small gift-wrapped conch shell I'd brought them as a souvenir from St. John years ago, so I could return it and have 'Good Jumbies' – an island version of 'good karma'. They also chipped in and bought me a beautiful gold bracelet made up of golden seashells linked together as a sort of retirement gift. I felt overwhelmed by their generosity. When my boss sprung the news at the party that I wasn't really leaving, some wise-aleck asked, "What do we have to give you so you'll really go?"

That last night before Bob left town should have been a quiet time together. Instead, long into the night we packed and repacked his car, trying to maximize the number of heavy and odd shaped boxes and goods that he could take. Boxes that couldn't be mailed due to postal restrictions had to go in one of our cars, or stay behind. Tensions and frustrations ran high. Fifteen phone call interruptions from those wanting to say a last good-bye didn't help. We fought over petty matters that were forgotten before the arguments waned. Bob's exacting approach to the final packing was unreasonable and I could do nothing 'right' that night. Even the cats avoided us. It was one last night of hell before Paradise.

Chapter Eight
The Paradise Expedition

Very early the next morning Bob left on his one way trek to Florida. It was anti-climatic for me. I felt left behind, and looked forward to Bob's promised nightly phone calls to bring me news of his progress. Six more weeks in New England stretched endlessly in front of me. My office workload was heavy, but my mind and my heart were on the road to Florida. I should have taken the day off. It was the last day before the Memorial Day weekend and the thought of spending it cleaning and packing while Bob had real life adventures was depressing. A couch, a bed and other furniture had to be given away to new homes. The checklist of moving tasks boggled my mind. Since last minute decisions were all mine, I intended to be superwoman and do it all in one weekend.

That afternoon I gave away the last of the dried flowers I'd been using as a wall hanging. It was symbolic. The sampler included seven bunches of flowers from my last garden a year earlier and was like saying good-bye to an integral part of my psyche. A flora and fauna book bought as part of our research for the move proved how little I knew about plants indigenous to St. John. I needed to see and touch them first hand to make any sense of these strange plants. With no real experience or understanding of my new environment, I'd be starting all over.

Bob's first day took him only as far as Delaware. A six-mile backup on the New Jersey Turnpike had slowed him down. Since he'd decided to take an uncharacteristic risk and not make advanced hotel reservations, Bob checked the Accommodations boards at each turnpike rest area starting mid-afternoon. Luckily he found a single motel under his fifty dollar per day lodging budget and secured their last available room for the night. Bob was stressed out when he phoned that evening.

"Nothing exciting." was Bob's judgement of his first day on the road. "But the hotel budget is making it hard to find a reasonable place to sleep."

It was a stilted conversation, as I tried to pry the details of his day out of him. Traffic, weather, pit stops, and plans for tomorrow were all on my mind. I reassured him that the travel budget was merely a guideline and that his safety and comfort were much more important than a few dollars. He sounded relieved and promised to keep a journal of his thoughts and activities and to phone me every night. With that, Bob ended the conversation.

I said nothing about the fifteen trips I'd made to the condo's dumpster that evening, making some progress in whittling down our worldly possessions. Nor did I tell him my decision to take a break and relax that weekend. Only fourteen hours in and I could not live up to my Superwoman image.

Each night I impatiently waited for the phone to ring and plotted Bob's progress on a map. The farther away he traveled the more communicative he became in sharing thoughts and experiences. Bob related mostly trivial and somewhat corny tidbits, but I ate them up. Sudden changes in the smells out his car window in southern Virginia where late spring flowers were in bloom and his descriptions of the wildflower patches in the Carolinas were intermingled with the restaurants Bob visited and the details of each meal. Where he dined meant little to me as I'd have two cats in my follow-up expedition and would be limited to fast takeout foods during daytime hours. Still I encouraged him, as I listened closely for some gem of information useful for my own trip south like road conditions and detours and where and why he'd decided to bed down each night.

Bob's arrival in Florida marked a change in the tone of his nightly calls. Anticipation was growing as he neared this milestone. I sent an overnight package to the hotel he'd booked in Ft. Lauderdale. Our new bank on St. John had sent automatic teller machine cards to my parents' address rather than holding them for him on St. John as we'd requested. I included some other minor items Bob left behind and probably didn't need. Bob's audible pleasure at the thought of getting a package from home turned me to mush.

I retrieved some small items of Bob's that had been destined for the garbage bin that night as a gesture of goodwill.

I called my landlady to inform her we'd be moving earlier than planned, and offered to split the remaining rent on the lease. Since she'd been adamant about the one-year lease, I expected the worst. But, she said that she and her husband had just sold their home and she'd be willing to let us off the hook and return our rental deposit if I could be out in mid-June. That was less than three weeks away and meant I'd then be homeless for two weeks before my own expedition was scheduled to depart. Why did I squander that long holiday weekend by taking a break? I would be paying for it dearly. Life became more chaotic.

In Ft. Lauderdale, Bob's expedition was also taking a traumatic turn. He attempted to check into the wrong hotel before discovering there were four with similar names in town and hadn't worn sunscreen religiously during the trip so his left arm was now beet red. The sticker shock of staying for once in a fine hotel unsettled Bob. It took an extravagant bottle of his favorite wine and a four-course dinner to calm him. It was deserved, Bob assured me. After dinner, it gave him the energy to empty essentials from his car, unpack and begin consolidating and throwing out excess baggage. True to form, Bob had continued to collect travel literature throughout his trip along with newspapers, comfort foods, etc. He'd filled all the wastebaskets in the room and still had maps, schedules and notes strewn across his bed when I called.

Bob told me he was trying to iron out the confusing logistics for the next day. Most major roads were under construction in the Ft. Lauderdale area and he hadn't a clue how to find the barge company. The ninety-degree temperature that day had made the sunburn on his arm from driving with the windows open even worse despite using an SPF-45 sunscreen all day. To add to his woes, I informed Bob that his flight and departure time from Miami to St. Thomas had been changed. The airline had left a phone message on our soon to be packed answering machine earlier that day. When I told Bob I'd be homeless soon, I got little sympathy. The only New England news that interested him was that I'd sent him an overnight package.

My husband survived that next day, and to his credit Bob even created a hand-drawn map to the barge company, complete with notes on all the detours so my trip would go a little smoother. He transferred all the gear he would need immediately in St. John to the rental car and made a test drive to the airport. That night, Bob was excited when he called. Within twenty-four hours he'd be in St. John and hopefully calling me from our new apartment.

The next day my thoughts were with Bob and I wished I could read his mind. Each time I looked at a clock I thought of his progress. He was on the way to the airport, on the plane to St. Thomas, and then he was on a shuttle van crossing the island. I tracked him in my thoughts as he arrived at the ferry dock in Red Hook and found a porter to help with his overflowing baggage. By my next glance at a clock I knew he'd arrived, found another porter and was likely in the process of renting a car. From that point forward, I lost any sense of what Bob was doing and said a prayer of thanks that he'd gone first. Did he find the apartment, or his new boss? Would he call me that night?

That night Bob did call, very agitated and with a lot of phone static. He'd arrived on St. John without incident. But just when my visions blurred, so had his progress. His expectations had been squashed.

"How's Paradise?" I asked innocently enough.

"It's not what we expected," he said. "There was a little mix-up with the apartment."

What happened?" I asked.

"There's more. I went to the Post Office and no packages have arrived." Bob sounded desperate. "Chuck said I sent them the wrong way and not to expect them for four to six weeks!" Who, I wondered was Chuck? Which boxes? Bob had sent some boxes for immediate use before he'd left New England, including his computer so we could e-mail each other and basics for the apartment like bed sheets and pillows. Before I could react, he continued.

"The place needs cleaning. There's no toilet paper, sheets, towels or anything and no screens in the windows and I'm getting eaten alive."

"Is the…" was as far as I got in response, before Bob cut in, even more agitated than before.

"I don't have time to talk," he said. "The phone isn't working right and I had to borrow a neighbor's – uh, Will's - cell phone to call you."

"What are you going to do?" I cut in.

"I don't know yet. Look, I'll try to call you tomorrow if I can find a phone. I'm going to have to sleep on the couch tonight and it's pretty raunchy. I've got to go. I'll call you when I can." And with that, a dial tone came onto the line and I was cut off. I hardly slept that night worrying about Bob and wondering why we chose to arrive separately. I felt helpless.

Two days later, the whole story came out. Bob's final leg to St. John was uneventful. No one questioned the ski bag filled with tiki lamps and other sordid items. The rental property manager met Bob at the ferry dock and helped carry the luggage down the block to his van, as the porter would only carry baggage to the end of the pier. Along the way, Bob was told a tale of woe about the cleaning of the condo or lack thereof. The property manager had hired a guy to do it the day before, but apparently he'd gone to the wrong place. Bob had to adapt until someone could clean it the next day.

The van was parked next to the Post Office, which perked up Bob. He asked for a little time to get his bearings before proceeding to the apartment, which the property manager willingly granted, as he had some errands to run himself. Bob made a quick stop inside the Post Office to pick up the boxes of emergency gear he'd sent ahead before he'd left New England. There was no mail of any kind waiting for him at General Delivery. He then sought out Chuck, his new employer at Bestech, to say he'd arrived and was ready for work. Then Bob related his adventures that day. Chuck relayed the sad news that the boxes of emergency goods and the computer probably wouldn't arrive for another month and suggested that everything be sent priority mail if we wanted to see it within a couple of weeks of mailing. Bob was told to take a couple of days to get settled in and then to contact him again to start work.

Back in the van, Bob and his host proceeded to the edge of town towards the apartment. The roads were steeper than Bob remembered. As the van climbed a hill known as Jacob's Ladder, he was told that it's a good thing we had four-wheel drive vehicles as the grade made it difficult to drive up when it rained.

I can only imagine Bob's state of mind by the time he crested the last hill to the new apartment. It was quite large, with a fantastic view overlooking Cruz Bay and St. Thomas in the distance. Built into a steep hill, the entire front provided unobstructed views quieted only by the floor length shutters that acted as doors. But there were no screens to keep bugs out. Keeping out rain meant keeping out air. The apartment was filthy, with furniture jumbled together and trash left over from a previous tenant.

Bob kept his thoughts to himself. I think he was in a state of shock. He asked for and got a ride back to town under the guise of picking up some essentials before the stores closed for the night. Bob bought a beer to calm his nerves, rented a car, then purchased drinking water, paper towels, toilet paper and cleaning detergent. Nowhere could he locate a place to purchase sheets and towels.

After the borrowed telephone and quick collect call home to me, things got a little better. The new neighbors took pity on Bob and loaned him a towel and a sheet for the couch and gave him some wine to mellow out before he headed off to a restless sleep. While Bob was mellowing, I was getting hysterical. I quickly located and moved two big boxes into my car. Inside were items luckily packed months ago - linens and dish detergent and lots of other things he could use now. The next morning I rushed to the Post Office and paid a fortune to make sure his life would get better by Monday.

Meanwhile, 'St. John Saturday' coincided with Bob's trip to Cruz Bay that morning. It was livelier than normal and he had an opportunity to touch base with local organizations and businesses and ponder on how he would ever fit in. He managed his first success, a Post Office box in our new company name. In one day. This would become a local legend, everyone told Bob on-island that day.

One night at the apartment had convinced my husband that I would not be happy living there. He began searching for an alternative abode that afternoon. My constant reassurances that I trusted his judgement in this area had paid off for me, while they tormented Bob. He checked at Connections, the newspaper, and even the dry cleaners looking for leads. Bob made appointments to visit available places the next day. Meanwhile, the apartment we were renting was being cleaned. By the time Bob returned in late afternoon it was better. He'd bought a bottle of wine as a neighborly thank-you for their help the night before and passed time with them getting ideas on how to get settled in quickly.

Bob called from a pay phone that night after dinner, much more upbeat than the night before. It was obvious that he was more relaxed. By the end of that conversation I was glad he had gone to St. John before I arrived with the cats in tow. Bob would be very busy for the next few days as he tried to settle in and prepare for our arrival. I suggested that he take some time off and go to the beach after looking for apartments the next day and that skip our nightly call the next night. He obviously needed a break and some time to enjoy the nicer side of Paradise.

When we finally talked that Monday evening, Bob's spirits were high. He'd found a new place for us to live. It was in a section called Century Hill, which I couldn't find on any map, but when he told me he could see the rental villa we'd rented on our last vacation from the front door, I was sold. In those two days, my wonderful husband had not only looked at four apartments, and secured one he thought I'd like, but he also managed to talk the original property rental manager into refunding all our monies including the deposit. In between Bob got his bank ATM card activated, went to a job interview on St. Thomas in case the job on St. John didn't work out, relaxed at a beach and bought food and supplies. He'd even taken pictures of the 'old' apartment and the new one he'd be moving into, paid a fortune to have the film developed immediately, and had them sent Express Mail in a care package which would arrive at my office by Wednesday. And, he'd gotten his laundry done. The two boxes I'd sent Express Mail that were waiting for him at the Post Office made his day. Wow! What a difference a couple of days made.

Back in New England, everything began moving forward with more speed than I thought possible. While Bob acclimated to St. John that week, mine was spent ridding myself of our worldly possessions. Now that I had an address for mailing purposes, I put our shipping plan in action. Each person who was to mail boxes to us received an envelope along with their boxes. In the envelope was a one-page flyer with our mailing address and step by step instructions on what to do and when. The envelopes also included blank insurance forms for the Post Office, hard cold cash to cover the shipping and insurance, a detailed list of the box contents including shipping weight, requested insurance amount, and total cost. I even included a self-stamped return envelope for them to mail us the Post Office receipts. I was leaving nothing to chance.

Every day before heading to work, I loaded my car with boxes and came home with it empty. Unfortunately, each delivery of boxes and envelopes required socializing as well. Convinced that I'd still be delivering boxes after the deadline to vacate the condo, I felt rushed and didn't enjoy each visit as much as I'd have liked.

The care package from Paradise lifted my spirits temporarily. In it were Bob's travel logs from his trip down the Eastern Seaboard to Florida, a home made street map to help me through the car-to-barge process, the photos he'd promised and even tourist literature to give out to friends. With newfound purpose, I emptied the condo room by room. As each one got down to the bare essentials of furniture, I cleaned one last time. Each night I was dog-tired, and anxious for Bob's call from Paradise to keep me motivated.

My second week continued like the first, and then it was moving time. I'd taken care or shutting down the utilities and the telephone and forwarded all our mail to St. John. Bob and I talked every evening on the logistics. I was down to those three pieces of furniture - a bed, a dresser and a couch. When my bed was taken by its new owner, I moved to the couch, but by the last night, I slept on the floor with a pillow and a featherbed that would go to a new home the day I left town. I'd managed to get all the box deliveries done and in the process had personally mailed twenty or so boxes to St. John. Most would go by parcel post, which meant I'd be in St. John before they arrived.

While I was closing down our life in New England, Bob was preparing the household for our arrival, ordering propane for the stove and getting the telephone connected. He cleaned and cleaned and finally figured out the new apartment had one drastic drawback. The amount of dust that accumulated in our condo in New England in a whole month was the amount gathered in a single day at our place in St. John. He even bought cat food and kitty litter, though we wouldn't be arriving for three more weeks.

Bob adjusted to the rhythms of island life as he worked his way through constantly growing lists of things to do. He picked up his car in St. Thomas, got it registered along with a new VI drivers' license, filled our apartment pantry with essentials, got a library card and made neighborhood friends. In between, Bob began work as a contractor for Chuck at Bestech, the computer company on St. John.

Up in New England I was staying with Birdie while I reconciled myself to the life we'd left behind. Our friends were now burdened with our life's possessions, while I had only two suitcases of clothes, two sets of travel supplies for the cats and two tool chests we couldn't bear leaving behind. There was barely room left in my car for Birdie and her two pieces of travel gear. Space for the two cats was a problem. It would be dangerous to leave them loose in the vehicle, but their travel carriers were too small and restrictive for the long days of travel ahead of us. I needed a way to separate the front and the back of the car, so they could have a little room to move around without causing a disaster. After numerous attempts, I hit on an idea that worked.

I bought duct tape, lots of Velcro, glue and bird netting (the kind you use to keep birds out of your ripening garden) and enlisted the help of my niece to put it all together. The netting was doubled over and the edges reinforced with duct tape. This doubly strong barrier was taped into place from the floor up, along the brace behind the front seats that held the doors in place. The top third was held in place with Velcro, so I could get into the back to reach the cats when necessary. A waterproof tarp covered the luggage and a soft blanket on top became our cats' bed for the duration. As she surveyed our work, my niece suggested that she could squeeze in the back to baby-sit the cats. It was with great reluctance that I squashed the idea. Birdie and I would be claustrophobic as it was for the whole trip.

My phase of the Paradise Expedition moved out with hardly a hitch. The travel logs Bob mailed me were a constant source of valuable information with their warnings of construction areas and mislead-ing signs. Challenges for Birdie and I came from very different sources. Unlike Bob before me, I'd attempted to make reservations for each stop along the route but in some areas no hotel or motel would allow animals. This was true of our first nights destination. We scouted for alternatives at rest area bulletin boards along the way until we gave up and just sneaked them into our preregistered 'no pets allowed' room for the night.

This took a well-coordinated effort with Birdie acting as lookout while I closed the car doors behind her, opened the top of the netting, and coaxed the little darlings into their travel bags. That first time was difficult, but I was smarter than my cats. With air vent flaps down, it appeared at a distance that Birdie and I were carrying ordinary gym bags. At least that was the case if one didn't look too closely and notice the bags seemed to have lives of their own. We felt like criminals as we sneaked the cats through the hallway, but at the same time we enjoyed the excitement after a boring day of driving.

Cleaning the room before we left, I hoped no one would know we'd broken any rules. We used temporary litter boxes that we brought with us and threw the used ones out each morning outside the hotel in the closest garbage bin we could find. It was hot, and difficult to stop during the day, as we couldn't leave the cats in the car alone in the heat wave covering the entire Eastern Seaboard. At rest stops Birdie and I took turns going inside and acting as cat chaperone and entertainer. Finding places to eat lunch was a challenge and we limited ourselves to fast food along the highway. We made a few wrong turns when we strayed off Interstate 95 for a change of scenery, but that made the drive more interesting. I don't think we added any mileage at all to the trip by detouring from the AAA recommended route, but the back roads took longer to navigate. The countryside away from the Interstate was worth it.

While we worked our way south, Bob was contemplating our future. It's true we both had jobs, but his was only panning out as a part-time endeavor to start and my long term prospects as a telecommuter seemed slim. With an on-island perspective, Bob researched any idea that came his way, from becoming a full time artisan to opening a bar to network consulting. He continued writing his travel logs, which took on a distinctly philosophical tone. In them he toyed with creative writing as he attempted to describe local sunsets.

"Describing a sunset is probably better left to some talented writer, but I'll take a stab at it. There is an interplay of many different shades of gray. There are gaps in the gray clouds where light grays pour through. All the while the silhouette of the islands are in the picture." For my husband this was pure poetry. His travel logs continued with pages detailing cultural differences he observed between the many layers of locals and tourists he saw on St. John. We were in two different Universes.

Time flew by. In South Carolina we couldn't resist the signs for unbelievably low warehouse prices on anything we could imagine right off the highway. A bathroom break turned into a quick shopping spree for Birdie and I, adding beach towels and snacks and even new towels to my overloaded luggage. It was a good thing that we didn't dare leave the cats unattended and our individual shopping sprees were limited to five-minutes. There was no space left in the car.

The cats were wonderful traveling companions. They stayed in the back, and although they took turns complaining for the first hour and the last hour of every day, in between they were no trouble at all. Except for that little incident in Georgia. My outdoor adventurer wanted out. He'd noticed a small gap in the bird netting that separated their temporary quarters from the front seat, not more than an inch wide. I was cruising down the highway and had just passed a slower vehicle. That's when he made his desperate break for freedom. Suddenly there was a shadow on my left side while on my right Birdie screamed.

Turning my head, I came face to face with my adventurer as he attempted to squeeze his huge body through the tiny gap in the mesh. I had no choice. With one hand, I firmly grasped his head and pushed him backwards, as I attempted to safely steer the car onto the highway shoulder. The cat was as shaken as I was. A little more duck tape convinced him that I was in charge and there would be no escapes to freedom before the expedition was over. My little princess helped the outdoor adventurer over his disappointment by licking his face and both were on their best behavior from that point onward. Birdie spent the afternoon looking constantly over her shoulder to make sure.

Nightly phone calls to Bob relayed our progress as he tried to provide remote advice for our next day's adventures. New neighbors were eager to answer any questions. Bob uncovered obstacles to local gardening. Undeterred he went to St. Thomas and bought big bags of soil and flowerpots in anticipation of my arrival. He had much faith in my ability to overcome any problems. New friends filled Bob in on past hurricanes, swimming pool maintenance problems, island folklore, and even car maintenance and food buying strategies. During odd hours, my husband managed to join the St. John Yacht Club and the St. John Action Committee. He signed on as a volunteer for the VI National Park and even became a member of the newly forming St. John Volunteer Rescue Squad.

Finally Birdie and I arrived in Florida feeling a sense of accomplishment and with a half day of free contingency time on our agenda.

The automobile was on its way to St. John, a rental car had been secured, and the cats were happily enjoying their 'pets allowed' suite for a luxurious two night stay.

Birdie suggested we spend the morning on a gambling boat so she could play a little blackjack and win some money to buy tourist trinkets on St. John. It made me feel naughty, but I needed that. We weren't prepared for the fun we had. Many senior citizens took advantage of these daily cruises to nowhere and the prices just couldn't be beat. For just more than the price of breakfast, we enjoyed a buffet with live music and were 'adopted' by some of the regulars as they passed on gaming tips to us novices. Birdie won enough money to pay for the cruise and all the souvenirs she wanted on St. John. A whole half day without the cats was a vacation in itself, but still I was panicked as we rushed back to the hotel only to find the little darlings sleeping away the day.

I was determined there would be no problems at the airport. My cats were each bought a 'ticket' that allowed them to travel as carry-on baggage under our seats. I'd convinced our veterinarian to provide a tranquilizer for each cat and I prayed that the Prozac he prescribed would be effective. Surprisingly they calmed down nicely and stayed that way until we landed on St. Thomas. Still, they managed to stay awake and aware through the whole ordeal.

Our arrival on St. Thomas was a letdown of sorts. I kept looking for the supposed Health Inspector to check our kitties' paperwork and to welcome them to the Island. No one approached us. I refused to ask anyone for help and decided to let well enough alone. It was a long hot walk to the baggage area. Bob was waiting there for us, but he was hard to recognize. Normally well groomed, his hair hadn't been cut since Massachusetts and he looked tired. He was glad to see us in one piece.

Yet, Bob saved most of his attention for the cats. They remembered him immediately and wanted out of their cages to sit in his lap. So while we waited patiently for our bags to depart the plane, my island husband sat against a far wall and sang softly to his pets. He looked like a native St. Johnian already. Having our own car to ride across St. Thomas from the airport was a unique treat. But, I was impatient to get to St. John, and hardly noticed the sites Bob pointed out. He'd already found all the supermarkets and department stores and the shortcuts across the island to the ferry dock in Red Hook.

There was a downside to this personalized tour. As Bob swung the car around and backed the car to within an inch of another vehicle on the barge to St. John, I knew this part of island life would not be glamorous. We were boxed in on all sides, with just enough room to open our car doors and stand on the car deck. There was a garbage truck on the barge, providing atmosphere. This was not a pleasant way for Birdie to see St. John for the first time.

"Follow me," said my husband, with a cat bag in tow. He proceeded to the back of the barge where a steel staircase led to a small operations deck. Up he went, without a backward glance.

Birdie and I had little choice but to follow. I went slowly as I was worried about losing my grip on the cat bag in my arms and dropping one of our precious cargoes overboard. Reaching the top, I walked around to the side, where Bob met me at a door. "Let's bring the cats inside here. It's air conditioned and they'll be happier." I got the distinct impression that I was merely an afterthought.

As the boat hit open water, I went outside. Birdie was already there. "This is great," she said.

"It's nothing like coming over on the regular ferry," I insisted, wanting her to understand how nice the trip to St. John normally was. "The ferries take you into a beautiful dock in Cruz Bay. It's so picturesque. But on this thing, we'll end up on the other side of the bay, in the Creek with the commercial vehicles where it's crowded and not very pretty." Birdie's first impressions mattered to me and I was sure she was disappointed.

"That's okay. This way is fine. You know what? I feel like Barbra Streisand in that movie on the tug boat in New York." When she stretched out her arms and let out a powerful note, I had to laugh. It would be okay. This was my best friend and she was trying to ease my concerns. It worked.

St. John Trivia

The most commonly recommended reading material for those considering a move to the USVI is "The Settler's Handbook" which is revised and updated regularly. It contains numerous facts, statistics, and listings of both government and private resources of benefit to the newcomer.

While inviting business investment in the islands, the book strongly suggests that unemployed people who are not independently wealthy should think twice about coming here.

Chapter Nine
Together At Last

An hour later, the vehicle rounded the last switchback and crested the ridge to our new apartment. By this point, Birdie's hands appeared to be permanently glued to the seat in front of her. The road was steep and rutted but Bob didn't seem to notice as he rushed to get us all home. I promised my friend she'd get used to the roads, but her teeth were clenched shut and only her eyes shouted her doubt. Miraculously our parking space was on a rare plot of flat ground. We gingerly exited the vehicle and tried to get the circulation back in our legs from the cramped ride while stalling the next surprise in store.

Both Birdie and I were skeptical about the apartment Bob had rented. Despite the photographs. After his last attempt at apartment hunting and the roach hotel he'd chosen in Massachusetts, who could blame us? While Bob held open the door with pride, I could see it in his eyes. I knew he knew I'd be hard to impress.

It was a nice place, if one ignored the warmth inside, the stacked boxes everywhere and the odd collection of furnishings the landlord had provided gratis. The apartment was indeed furnished as advertised, but the decor was 'early college' at best. The bottom floor consisted of a tiny kitchen with hurricane-scarred appliances, a small bathroom, a dining/living area with a cathedral ceiling leading to sliding doors and a concrete railed porch. There was also a small guestroom, without a closet, that had a sliding door that opened to the other end of the porch. A spiral stairway albeit filthy, led down to the postage-stamp sized swimming pool in the drought starved garden area below. Upstairs, a loft area opened up to the small master bedroom with a tiny balcony and another bathroom. A light layer of dust was everywhere and the windows were filthy, but at least these windows had real glass in them.

After a quick tour I announced, "It has potential". Birdie gave me a long look, but put on a supportive smile. She knew when to stay out of our domestic affairs. Bob had taken the rest of the day off from work and spent the next few hours filling me in on details of our new life that I forgot within minutes. I had no reference points to keep up with the myriad of names and places he described. The household disarray kept dragging my thoughts to other matters. Birdie spent hours hiding in the crowded shabby guestroom. Perhaps we were all overtired. Everyone was asleep by nine o'clock. The cats wisely chose the guestroom and Birdie for the night.

My first full day in Paradise was to be a vacation day for everyone. It was July 4th and St. John Carnival activities were at their peak. We intended to avoid Carnival at all costs because I longed for quiet solitude after frantic months of moving preparations. Bob, anxious to go to the beach as always, was very willing to accommodate. And so our first morning was absolutely perfect. He drove us directly to the north shore beaches and avoided town completely. We passed the fondly remembered plywood fork in the road sign on the way and even made a few stops for Birdie to take photos.

Birdie was initiated into the world of snorkeling at Francis Bay on the north shore. It was Bob's favorite beach and as he predicted there were only two or three other people within sight. It was a good thing as my friend was on the large side and was self conscious about being seen in a bathing suit. While she professed to be a good swimmer, I encouraged her to be cautious and take breaks often. Once Birdie saw the aquarium like environment, my warnings and her self-consciousness had little meaning. She had to be coerced into returning to land to rest and unpickle her skin in between adventures.

That very first morning Birdie swam unknowingly from Francis Bay over to little Maho Bay. She'd never heard of Ethel McCully or the others who'd followed in her path. Someday that morning's adventure may be Birdie's undoing, but we didn't have the nerve to tell her our suspicions. By mid afternoon our meager picnic lunch was long gone and we were ready for some refreshments. Congratulating ourselves for having avoided the Carnival Parade scheduled for that morning, Bob agreed to drive us to Mongoose Junction in Cruz Bay for a welcome cocktail.

We came into town from the north shore blissfully unaware. As we topped the last rise, the view gave way to the beautiful downtown harbor stretched below us on our right. But our attention was drawn to the chaotic sight on the road directly ahead. It was lined by cars on both sides, going all the way down to town. Trucks were trying to back up the hill while others were trying to go down. No one was making much progress and everyone was blowing his horn and using plenty of body language. It was nuts.

Bob snapped and reverted to a past lifetime as a Boston city driver. He barged his way past drivers going both directions, impervious to his female passengers' screams until he could go no further. A wall of people and an angry policeman stopped him. Undeterred, Bob backed up and swung the car's rear end into a minute patch of weeds on the shoulder of the road just wider than his vehicle. He came to a stop only when his front end was completely off the pavement.

I was angry. My friend was panicked. Bob didn't understand our problem. He was again the nice person we'd been driving with on the north shore road. But now, we were stuck in the middle of the height of Carnival. The parade had begun hours late, which we should have expected. It was in high gear with over ten thousand people crowed in the few blocks that normally held hundreds. We tried to get into the spirit but we just weren't prepared for the crush of humanity.

We retraced our route as the parade winded down and took a circuitous route back to the apartment where we watched the fireworks from our porch on that final night of Carnival. The next evening we watched the sunset and then the nightly show of lights on St. Thomas in the distance. The view was just as spectacular as the night before, but in a quiet sort of way. The three of us went to beach hopping that weekend. On the long walk to Salt Pond Bay, Bob gave us a lecture on the flora and the fauna. I received my own first hand experience when I took a quick side trip to a portable toilet near the beach and found a huge furry brown spider waiting to say hello. Birdie declined to check it out first hand.

Bob did most of the daily chores that first week. Birdie and I were happy to leave everything in his hands as a reward for surviving our expedition south. Our cats also enjoyed the good life. They seemed to realize their long ordeal was behind them. The outdoor adventurer began his explorations quickly. Within days he'd caught and killed his first gecko and he purred all night. Our little princess hid much of the time under a bed but occasionally made surprising forays outside. Within days she'd deemed the outside porch a part of her living space and had even taken a brave belly walk around the entire building. I was forgiven for their ordeal travelling to Florida in the back of my GEO Tracker.

My car didn't arrive for nine long days. We had forgotten to take into consideration a delay caused by the July fourth holiday which coincided with Carnival on St. John. Bob needed his car for work so I got a rental vehicle for a few days. I needed to get around town to run the small errands that couldn't wait. That added mobility provided Birdie and me with a chance to explore the island together as only two women could. She seemed more relaxed with me driving, but her white knuckles told a different story. And there was no way I could convince her to get behind the steering wheel and try driving on the left side of any road. It didn't help when I insisted on a visit to Lamshure Bay with its remote privacy and ruins and tidal pools. I wanted to show her my own favorite spot to while away a day. The steep four-wheeled drive dirt road was a necessity that Birdie survived with a clenched jaw. Thank goodness Birdie and I were such good friends.

By the end of every day we were exhausted. Each day boxes arrived at the Post Office bringing unpacking chores in the early evening hours. Although I started out committed to make Bob unpack everything, I quickly decided it was better that I lead the effort since many were boxes I'd mailed myself before leaving New England. Bob loaded the empty containers into his vehicle and brought them to the dumpster a half mile away, which helped to balance the scales. By the end of the week, our apartment was filled with our things, but not all were goods we needed right away. Those boxes were somewhere in the Atlantic Ocean – I hoped. Birdie just shook her head in amusement at our chaos.

Confiscating the dining room table for a computer desk, my girlfriend helped me set up some dedicated office space for myself which Bob would consider sacred territory. Having my best friend there for my first week on-island was fun, but it had prevented reality from setting in. I went back to work the day Birdie departed. My two-week 'vacation' that started with the drive from Massachusetts was history. Beach adventures would now be limited to weekends or the occasional holiday.

Very quickly, the difficulties of being a very remote telecommuter became apparent. No firm projects had been assigned to me and much time was spent trying to establish firm working hours while juggling constant use of our single poor quality phone line, switching between on-line computer use and long distance phone calls. During certain hours it took up to ten tries to access the 800 number connection to my company's headquarters. We lost power for just a few minutes at a time on a regular basis. I was productive, but it took excessive effort on my part. A month passed before I felt comfortable with the situation.

Three days into my new work routine, my automobile arrived on St. Thomas and I was faced with the task of retrieving it alone. In Cruz Bay, I located the tax office and paid for my vehicle. Then I proceeded to locate the Motor Vehicle Department for a one-day permit to bring my vehicle on a barge without a proper vehicle inspection sticker. With paperwork, lots of cash, and a hand-drawn map from Bob, I took a ferry, then a bus and then a walk to the shipping company on the docks in St. Thomas.

I filled out paperwork at the shipping company and then caught another bus to the US Customs office. A long walk back, with nary a bus in sight, got me some stamped paperwork and the keys to my car. I managed to drive directly across town to the Red Hook barge dock by instinct alone. Then I faced the stress of backing my car onto the barge while juggling for position with fifteen other anxious drivers. It was an ordeal. The regularly scheduled barges were the sole way to get a vehicle between the islands and if the barge filled before my car could wedge its way on board, I'd be left to stew on the dock for an hour before the next departure. I made it. Immediately upon arrival in Cruz Bay, I headed to the Motor Vehicle Inspection lane. The process had taken over half the day so far and I was not in a patient mood.

Parked in the Inspection Lane next to a trailer marked with a small official looking sign, I went inside to present my paperwork. I expected quick approval, and was shocked when five minutes later I was being yelled at by the inspector and told that my brake lights weren't working, nor were my back-up lights. A stern warning was followed by dispensation until the next morning when I was told to return with the lights working. Two repair shops determined that there was nothing wrong with my car. And, I'd learned not to follow the inspector's directions verbatim if I wanted my parking lights to go on. Late into the evening, I tried to make up the work hours I'd missed.

When I heard that we could give back any of the furniture or other items our landlord had supplied, I was ecstatic. It wasn't that I was ungrateful, but Bob and I had lots of our own things that I would rather use, and we were cramped for space. A chair and many kitchen utensils were quickly removed, followed by linens and framed pictures and a host of other items. Our apartment seemed spacious for the next week, until our own mailed goods arrived in enough quantity to make it all cluttered again.

We needed bookshelves. Three separate times Bob brought home a small bookcase purchased on St. Thomas to accommodate the growing library mailed from New England. Smugly I guessed he'd misjudged just how many books and computer manuals he'd packed. The truth made me more humble. The bookcases had to make their way from the store in St. Thomas to the bus to the ferry to the car on St. John. My narrow point of view had been expanded. A St. John yard sale yielded our fourth bookcase that I quickly confiscated and filled within minutes for my home office needs.

Now that I had my own wheels on island, I made an effort to drive to town each day to pick up mail and if lucky, packages. On the return trips I stopped to survey the markets for fresh foods. It was a chore to get myself away from the computer and the phone to take this break part way through the day. No matter when I left, during that hour my boss would decide to call or some work emergency would occur which required my personal attention.

Food shopping quickly became my primary social activity. Whenever I checked the stores for fresh foods, I often discovered new acquaintances doing the same. There was little that couldn't be found or bought, but it took much more effort than on the continent. Each of the small grocery stores on the island had its own idiosyncrasies. One was relatively reliable for vegetables but another had a better selection of canned goods while a third was the place to shop for meat...sometimes. Prices on some items changed daily and most were exorbitant. I began to get connected to the human telegraph system on island when it comes to food. A surprise phone call or whisper from a neighbor told me the meat truck was just seen headed to one of the markets outside its normal schedule, or there was fresh fish being sold on the dock, or a load of good looking cherries (!) was just unloaded at another market. Within an hour or two, no sign remained that any of these good things had happened.

Two short weeks after I started telecommuting, I had to fly back to New England on business. Three hectic hours back at my company's headquarters caused my new life in Paradise to fade in memory in that way vacations do. In the hallways, everyone wanted to know what living on St. John was like. I could only shrug and smile and wish I were there. After long workdays, my evenings revitalized me with rushed visits to my mom or shopping trips to pick up emergency items that my husband couldn't find locally at a reasonable price. I brought back a knapsack full of fresh corn on the cob to share with new island friends. There was nothing to compare with fresh New England corn in the Virgin Islands. The blast of hot island heat stepping off the plane in St. Thomas was welcome, though. This was my home now. It was a good feeling.

Before August was over, island peculiarities had become my norm. The local donkeys that are such a quaint tourist attraction became mere road obstacles to avoid. My automobile was constantly covered with a thick layer of dust and I'd begun to think of mud as the color of my car. No longer did I look down on the typical island vehicles that were inevitably dented on all four sides from mysterious sources. Baying goats were no longer confused with hidden babies crying out for help. Sometimes I even bayed back at them. And yes, I was even clued in on the local lore surrounding Moses and his cows.

It seems that Moses, a major landowner and farmer on the island, let his cows loose to free range wherever and whenever they wanted. These huge beasts were a regular nuisance on the only major road crisscrossing the island and were considered a safety hazard by government officials. Often when a resident discovered a new dent on their vehicle, they attributed it to being hit by one of Moses cows. By my own limited count, twenty-three people swore their car had faced this fate within the past thirty days. Either Moses had cows that were indestructible to withstand all those direct hits, or he had the miraculous ability to multiply his herd on a regular basis. At the time, I just couldn't accept that there were a lot of crooks on St. John taking out their petty frustrations on poor Moses. Regardless, his cows were a legend I began share with our off-island friends.

Most of my own encounters with Nature that first summer were limited by the confines of my home office. I learned about poisonous caterpillars, spiders, and lizards of every kind after experiencing them firsthand thanks to my cats. Unfortunately, while my cats seemed to believe that lizards were an Epicurean delight, their little stomachs thought differently. My downstairs neighbor, Karen, told me to be patient as the cats would soon learn to leave the heads alone and stop vomiting their catch. Nice. Surrounded by the exotic scenery, I thought it was pretty neat to live in a place where huge termite nests nestled in trees, eating all the rotten wood to minimize the likelihood of forest fires. Until, that is, my husband and I encountered firsthand a nighttime termite swarm.

This disaster first struck two months after the move. It was a beautiful tropical night with showers the previous two days making everything smell fresh and clean. Our screened doors were closed and lights were on all over our apartment. I noticed a few flying insects at first, and thought nothing of it. After all, we lived in the tropics and there were always ways for the occasional bug to get in. Within a half-hour we had a big problem.

"There's some kind of ants crawling everywhere in here", Bob said.

There were hundreds - on the floors, the walls, and the furniture. Bob went outside on the porch to retrieve some bug spray.

"Hey, there's thousands of little wings on the floor out here." Checking the living room floor, I found more wings. "Remember that book we read that said a sure sign of termites was a mound of fallen wings?" he asked.

I never thought I'd need that information. We lived in a very well built concrete condo that was well maintained. "Termites?" I asked timidly.

"Termites" was all he said as we both realized we had no idea what to do about it.

Within minutes our house was filled with thousands of these little ant-like creatures, some of them flying with wings still attached. The situation had gotten out of hand. They were on the walls, the floor, the furniture and even us. It seemed every minute there were more bugs climbing and flying around the apartment. Bob and I swatted and killed thousands of bugs without exaggeration. Even when we thought they were all dead, we found more, especially near light sources. It took hours to kill the majority of these pests. Our cats thought it was all great fun. We slept fitfully that night and yes, I had nightmares. The next morning, the only reminder of the evening's disaster was the occasional dead bug we'd killed but missed in our rushed cleanup the night before.

We mentioned our little bug adventure to neighbors and acquaintances and discovered we were not alone in our adventure. Bob's boss, Mark, had ridden his motorcycle right into a swarm on his way to

Fish Bay and got a helmet full. A neighbor told us his car headlights were covered with dead bugs in the morning. The more experienced told us, "Just shut off all the lights when it happens again - and it will". The termites had been washed out of their homes by the earlier rains - their fallen wings were a sure indication. And one we'd never ignore again. It would be an event that would repeat itself each year, so we would have to learn to adapt.

Bob decided it was important that we play by the rules laid down by the fine government of the Virgin Islands. He was determined to get a business license for his work as a contractor. At best, it was an overly complicated process. Filling out forms, finding documentation and searching for the proper government offices on St Thomas to submit it all took effort. While my husband was proud that he'd completed the process in only a few days, a month later Bob received a letter denying the license. There was no 'proof' on file that we'd paid Federal taxes to the Virgin Islands for the previous six years. The forms had clearly stated this was a 'new license' we were requesting, but that made no difference. Only copies of our US Federal Tax returns sufficed to get past the hurdle. Since the records were in storage over two thousand miles away, it was quite an ordeal.

Perhaps that's why some on-island folks, originally from the U.S. mainland, didn't bother with all the red tape of business licenses unless they got caught. We were appalled to discover that many didn't even bother with income taxes. It took Bob five queries to find the first soul who did. And that person used off-island accountants to handle all the mess. Like self-righteous coeds out to change the world, my husband and I were determined to pay our dues, register to vote, and make a difference. We would be part of the solution, not the problem.

Some newcomers from the mainland had a 'third world mentality' when it came to their favorite food or other luxury items. We met someone who loved pineapple yogurt. Whenever she saw it, she'd buy whatever the store had, leaving the shelf bare. I discovered the culprits who did the same thing with coffee ice cream, Pad Thai noodles, and prepped pizza dough. The stores couldn't plan for these weird fluctuations in purchases. Once in a while Bob or I stocked up on these very items, just to use for bartering. And that's how we too became part of the problem.

Bob started out buying coffee ice cream to bribe our neighbor, Andre, into helping us with some fix-up projects around the apartment. This neighbor, we'd been told, was addicted to the stuff. One day we tried the ice cream ourselves and we liked it. Then every store on the island ran out of that flavor. A stranger, seeing me head down in the freezer at Tropicale Market while I looked in vain for a hidden pint one day, took pity. She spied a pint of "Haagen-Dazs Coffee Mocha-Chip" I had discarded and said we'd like it even better. We did. Bob and I became addicted.

Soon there was no more coffee mocha-chip ice cream to be found anywhere. It was awful. Nothing else could satisfy our taste buds like a single spoonful of this stuff. Plain coffee ice cream now tasted bland and was only enjoyed after weeks without the added jolt of mocha-chips. It could easily be found on St. Thomas, but it was difficult to get ice cream back home to St. John without staging a major production.

Bob hunted for the ice cream distributor on St. John, hoping to convince him to keep the local markets stocked with our preference. When Bob caught up with the ice cream dealer one day, he was filling a store's cooler with cherry vanilla and without any coffee mocha-chip in sight.

"If you like that Haagen Dazs coffee stuff, I have something even better you'll like," whispered the ice cream man, as he led Bob to his van. "Try this," he said, whipping out his personal stash of "Ben & Jerry's Coffee, Coffee BuzzBuzzBuzz!" ice cream.

Bob brought home two precious pints. This was mean stuff. A couple of spoonfuls of this espresso blend were all it took to satisfy at first. It was so good, that even adding a scoop of coffee or plain vanilla ice cream didn't diminish the taste. In fact, a late evening snack required 'cutting' the "Coffee, Coffee, BuzzBuzzBuzz!" with vanilla if we wanted to get to sleep at night. When our two pints ran out, we couldn't find it anywhere, nor our trusty coffee mocha-chip alternative, or the dealer. Bob and I went through serious withdrawals. The ice cream man was sighted only fleetingly the next few months, which was a good thing as we weaned ourselves back to sanity. A pint of ice cream cost more than double the price of a bottle of rum on St. John, but we stopped our downward spiral of addictions before it came to that. Eventually we discovered the ice cream dealer also played in a musical band around the island and once we heard him play, we forgave him for feeding our temporary insanity.

My peers in the States often commented that I probably sat at the pool all day with a cell phone by my side soaking up the heat. There was heat, but it came from the hot sun pounding on the apartment all day. Ceiling fans turning overhead provided minimal relief. Friends insisted that our apartment was abnormally hot compared to others on the island, but I doubted them. The constant trade winds kept it bearable as long as the windows were open. Island wisdom has it that the trade winds bring dust and sand all the way from the Sahara Desert on a daily basis and I came to believe it quickly.

Only a year earlier I'd been complaining about dirt and dust caused by our septic tank replacement. What had seemed like an insurmountable problem paled compared to the daily influx I now faced. This summer brought the added joy of occasional soot arriving courtesy of the volcano on Montserrat, hundreds of miles away. Every morning I swept the floors and dusted and when the heat built up by mid afternoon, I wedged open the front door for five minutes so a rush of wind could cool it down while I worked. If the winds were strong, clumps of dust imbedded in the fans fell to the floor like little bugs. A five-minute break to sweep away the new layers of dust always followed.

Bob was experiencing his own work adventures. At least once a week he visited clients on St. Thomas and he was getting to know everyone and every place on both islands. He was learning the computer repair business from the ground up but didn't seem to mind. Still, Bob's work didn't quite keep him as busy as I'd hoped, as this was the quiet season in the islands. He got paid only for billable work and hadn't built up a backlog of work to carry him through the slow times. Too often my husbands day was done long before my own workday was over and I'd jealously see him down at the pool living the life my peers dreamed about.

We started to notice that people walking along the roadside both here and on St. Thomas were often carrying tree branches loaded with leaves and some kind of nut or fruit on the end. Curiosity led to questions and research on Caribbean plant life. We learned that the people were carrying branches from the genip tree, as this much-favored fruit was in season. One Saturday we saw a group of young people surrounding a tree near a beach in the VI National Park They were encouraging one of their crowd who was high in the branches and reaching towards a fat branch hanging heavy with fruit.

"Are those genips?" I asked. All eyes turned towards me as I rushed to correct my rudeness of jumping right into a conversation with a question. Once I restarted with a 'Good Morning', they confirmed my guess and I countered with "I've never tried any but I hear they are wonderful. We've just move here and do you think I might try one?"

With a single smile, the teenagers grinned. One gave me a small branch and showed me how to split open the outer shell with my teeth and get at the small amount of pulp surrounding an overly large seed. My face lit up with a grin as I savored my first genip. To me it tasted like a cross between a grape and a melon. The sweet taste was a perfect counterpoint to the salty aftertaste of hours spent beachside. One genip was hardly satisfying - after five more, I was in love. It became my favorite fruit.

Many people on-island walked long distances daily and relied on the kindness of others to catch a ride when tired or in a hurry. Even before genip season, I'd become accustomed to stopping at the side of the road to give others rides on my daily treks to town. Picking up hitchhikers is something I was trained from an early age not to do, but on St. John I felt safe. As a result, I made lasting acquaintances, got invited to share refreshments, viewed homes in process of being built, learned island folk lore and history, and most important, gained the pleasure that comes from helping others.

Much of the real news on-island didn't get reported in the local newspapers. For example, a small plane crashed on the north side of the island one day. Yet there was no newspaper article. I looked for weeks. Since the incident occurred on Federal property in the VI National Park, I was told the Park Service was under no obligation to report the news. While I learned lots of the local gossip from hitchhikers, my best source of information for what really had happened on a weekly basis came from, of all people, Bob.

One of the first things Bob had done after arriving on St. John was to join the fledgling St. John Rescue group. During the summer they held weekly meetings at the National Park Visitors Center which was the workplace for a couple of members. Not only was he learning first aid and critical rescue skills, but he was also getting an earful of little anecdotes and the sometimes-bizarre details of incidents that had occurred on the island during the previous week. Through him I learned much of the real news and rumors that never made it into print.

On Friday nights, I was able to confirm even the wildest stories through my own growing grapevine. Back in New England we'd always ended a stressful workweek with a quiet early Friday night at home, gearing up for a weekend of relaxation. Here Friday night was the night to cut loose. Everyone it seemed managed to party on that night, even if his or her jobs required getting up at five o'clock the next morning. Bob and I tried to take part, as it was a good way to meet other locals. Inevitably we were ready to pack it in by nine o'clock at night when many were just gearing up for a long night of fun. Still, the neighbors and new friends we met on these excursions enjoyed sharing their opinions of the latest St. John new flashes.

Our landlords, Moe and Bev, took us under their wing and treated us to a powerboat ride to Jost Van Dyke, a sparsely populated island in the British Virgin Islands. We spent the afternoon at the Soggy Dollar Bar, so named because until recently the only way to reach it was by boat or by swimming and most folks paid with wet dollar bills. These kind folks were the ones who had convinced Bob to join the St. John Yacht Club, a loose social organization compared to the smaller but more sailor-intensive Coral Bay Yacht Club. They made sure we were getting flyers in the mail for the regular SJYC parties and introduced us to lots of locals, including some who would become our closest friends on-island. An invitation to join Moe and Bev on St. Thomas for festivities following an annual marlin fishing competition opened our eyes to the details of this rich man's sport and as a bonus we saw our first mega-yacht up close.

Most 'excitement' in our lives was rather mundane by mainland standards. Regularly we had car problems. The recent age of our vehicles and our constant attention to preventative care made little difference. Bob had bought maintenance books for each of our cars just in case experienced mechanics were difficult to find when the inevitable occurred. But books were of minimal help when replacement parts weren't available. And books rarely mentioned the kind of trauma caused by local road and environmental conditions.

Bob became an expert at cleaning wires, testing electrical connections and tightening bolts. Usually the strange advice received from friends, neighbors, and yes, even local mechanics, worked and the sick vehicle was fixed with just a little muscle power. We were not alone. Mysterious car ailments were the norm for everyone. In the States, a breakdown would have put me into frenzy. Here, it brought only a shrug. As a two vehicle household, Bob and I were lucky and a cut above most others. We often loaned one car out when others had car problems and needed to run emergency errands.

The flow of boxes from New England had slowed to an occasional delivery. It was a relief after fourteen boxes arrived on a single day, prompting our tiny Post Office to take the extraordinary step to call our home and inform us of the arrival. Bob faithfully checked off each box in the *Paradise Expedition Manual,* while I cut open the boxes to retrieve our life. Bob remained a junk mail junkie. A rare day passed when he didn't receive mail of some kind. Unfortunately, his regular stock of magazines ended up cluttering the apartment rather than the trash bins half a mile away. Occasionally he could be persuaded to drop unwanted catalogs off at Connections in town where a bin was provided for this purpose. Sadly, he often returned home with alternate catalogs some other spouse had managed to get rid of.

I had big plans for Paradise, but there was so much I wanted to do, it was difficult to find a starting point. Eventually I hoped to become a clay artisan though my experience was minimal, and then there was the book I wanted to write and get published. Volunteering time reading to young children and assisting at the VI National Park were my philanthropic goals. There were also hiking trails, remote beaches and historical ruins I wanted to explore. And I wanted a garden to call my own.

In the evenings, I began to work with Polymer clay, working miniature island images into the art form known as millifore. After a few tries the palm trees, turtles and geckos came out without distortion, as I fashioned medallions threaded with leather strips. A vision of a profitable St. John Saturday danced in my mind. Bob particularly liked a fish medallion I made, and took to wearing it around town as part of his casual work attire. He came home one night and asked me to make a dolphin one for a business acquaintance at one of the resorts.

Weeks later the dolphin medallion was delivered gratis, and surprisingly Bob returned home with my first commission. Two hundred medallions to be used for a marketing promotion at the resort. They weren't needed until late fall and that seemed like a very reasonable schedule. I was an artisan. My November target for a St. John Saturday would coincide nicely.

On the occasional evening and weekend morning, Bob and I took to the trails and each outing improved my stamina and increased my desire to learn more about my newfound home. We even made it to the top of America Hill and its ruins I'd seen from beach level for years. Getting there was an ordeal, not because of the ruggedness or trail length, but because of the wild lime bushes and 'ketch-an-keep' plants that had overgrown this closed trail. The scratches and thorns imbedded in my arms and legs would teach me what the VI National Parks "Trail Closed" sign could not. They'd closed the trail for our own safety. Bob came away mostly unscathed, as he had conned me into blazing the trail ahead while he walked behind under the guise of pacing his hiking strides to my slower efforts.

Whenever we went to Lamshure Bay on the south shore we inevitably saw three or more white tailed deer near the dirt roadway on the final stretch before the beach in late afternoon. The surprise was that many locals who'd lived on our tiny island for twenty years had never caught a glimpse of these creatures. I'm also told there's also wild boar and even a one-day hunting season. The fact that I've never met anyone who's seen a boar on St. John doesn't mean it's not true.

A business trip to San Antonio and then Atlanta interrupted the late summer island rhythm. My productivity had greatly increased and I was working forty to fifty hours a week, though getting paid as a part-time worker. While traveling the work hours jumped even higher. But I was happy to do it since my company was accommodating my life-style and I knew that eventually the hours would lessen. This trip's return landing in St. Thomas was even sweeter than the one a month before. Another snorkeling weekend was about to begin and my life-style had become routine.

Before summer's end, Bob announced that snorkeling each weekend was too much effort. He'd begun to insist that we take at least one float with us on our weekend excursions to the beach. Instead of snorkeling, Bob immediately headed for the water with float in hand, then plopped down to soak up the rays while tourists took photographs of him from the National Park provided roadside scenic overlooks in the distance.

He was quite a sight. We'd received our dual-purpose heavy-duty floats for Christmas presents before our move. These toys were designed to work as sleds or toboggans sliding down snow covered hills with their sturdy side handles and snowflake patterned design emblazoned with the words 'Authentic Snow Gear'. The floats were likely designed to be flipped over in summer so that the plain colored smooth plastic side would provide a smooth floating surface. Regardless, Bob preferred to have the 'snow gear' emblem showing on the surface, just to amuse tourists with telephoto lenses.

Soon, I joined him in this weekend fun and discovered two snow floats was the maximum my little car could transport. We decided that amusing the tourists was a responsibility like our offering to take group pictures for tourists with their own cameras. Snorkeling was now kept to days when we had extra energy to spare. Some of our neighbors, although surrounded by water, only rarely made it to a beach at all. It seemed we'd avoided any disastrous interruption in our routing, until the phone rang late one Sunday night.

St. John Trivia

The only truly "native" mammals living on St. John today are a handful of bat species! All of the others - including mongooses, rats, and donkeys - were brought to the island by boat. Small white-tailed deer, originally brought to the island in the late 1700's, have adapted well and can often be found around sunset near Big Lamshure Bay in the south part of the island.

Goats are found in their greatest number on the east end of St. John, where they often lay in groups along roadways to take naps. Donkeys, until recently a common form of transportation, roam almost everywhere.

Chapter Ten
Disruption in Paradise

Fate had dealt my brother in New Hampshire a lousy hand. He needed a new kidney. My sister-in-law relayed the news. As a diabetic, Joe was a poor candidate for dialysis. While I'd heard hints that he wasn't feeling well, Joe's health went into a drastic downward spiral during the latter half of the summer. His wife asked that night on the phone if I would consider being a donor if it ever became a necessary last resort.

A transplant was not an option for 'someday', but his real need in the next year. The waiting list for kidney donors was averaging three years at the time, and his chances for survival if he waited that long were very slim. My sister-in-law was being tested as the most likely donor and all her tests pointed in the right direction. I was happy they'd found a quick solution. Without hesitation but with confidence that I would never be needed, I agreed to be their last resort.

It was a surreal conversation that seemed as foreign to my daily reality as the evening television news on world affairs. On St. John, the Flamboyant trees were blooming. They arched across roads and paths like flaming clouds resting on a lining of emerald green foliage. At Francis Bay, a five-foot iguana came by to visit and drink water from the makeshift container I held in my hand. That very day I'd spied my first pomegranate tree heavy with fruit in someone's fenced yard and smiled all the way to town. From the porch that night the full moon's reflection shimmered on the waters separating us from St. Thomas and the beauty of it made me breathless. Yet, my brother and I looked at the same moon that night.

In early September, I was asked to fly to Boston with the rest of the immediate family for a 'family meeting' with my Joe's doctors. Joe's condition had worsened. Luckily, I had a business trip scheduled for that week, and could easily take one day of vacation time for the meeting. Janine had continued to test well as a potential donor and we were all anticipating the discussion of a timeline for her donation, how we could be supportive as a family, and what the odds were of a successful transplant. The meeting opened with a bombshell.

The hospital staff had just come from their own private meeting where they'd disqualified my sister-in-law as a potential donor. She'd had breast cancer over fourteen years earlier and although there was no sign of reoccurrence, there was a theoretic possibility that she could pass a hidden cancer cell on to Joe through the transplant. It was a smaller likelihood than the remote chance that she'd die during the routine transplant surgery, but malpractice concerns dictated prudence. Unified, the doctors reiterated their final decision to the entire family. Under no circumstances would they take her kidney. I felt sorrow as Janine sat in disbelief with tears in her eyes. Her hopes for a quick improvement in their quality of life had been deflated. In a split second, the mood of the room changed.

All eyes in the room shifted towards me, where the enormity of the situation was slowly sinking in. The rest of my family had been summarily rejected for a variety of medical conditions and I was Joe's only hope. Still no one even knew if I was compatible. It was not the forum I would have liked to begin a serious dialog on the matter so I kept quiet as other family members asked questions. I learned of the twelve to sixteen inch incision, the hospital and recuperation time, and the likelihood one of my ribs would have to be removed to gain access to the kidney. It was all a blur. This was no longer a meeting about Joe and his condition, but one about me.

My husband had not flown up to join in the family meeting with the doctors. I felt comfortable that I could relay the facts and findings later. Bob's contracting job at Bestech was just stabilizing and his evenings were filled with a specialized first aid training course as a requirement for the St. John Volunteer Rescue group. Besides, my sister-in-law was to be the donor and I was just there to lend support. How I wished Bob had insisted on tagging along.

As the conference was ending, I finally found my voice. "Uh, it seems like we're all talking about what is probably going to happen to me, since I'm the only possible candidate in the room. But I haven't even been tested yet." With inspiration I added "And I live in the Virgin Islands, and I'm only here for a few days." I don't know what I'd expected to happen, but it certainly wasn't what followed.

Within seconds I was shaking hands with my brother's kidney specialist and trying to keep pace with the man as he rushed through the hallways and down the street while querying me on my medical history. He wanted to begin testing immediately to determine my viability as a candidate. With amazement I was ushered to his private office and led directly to an available examination room as the physician kept up his barrage of questions without a single break.

Ten minutes later the initial exam was almost complete. Given a specimen jar, I was asked apologetically to walk across the filled waiting room to provide a quick urine sample in the bathroom beyond. Entering the waiting room in only my medical johnny, I discovered to my distinct embarrassment my entire family talking up a storm, city blocks away from where I'd left them. My brother Don from Pittsburgh was upset that he'd been dismissed as a candidate without a detailed examination and the whole family was loudly trying to calm him down. I was freaked out that everyone considered me the perfect candidate with just similar generalized knowledge but I kept quiet and hardly broke stride as I rushed past, hoping the bathroom was where I'd been told. I wanted to hide.

The preliminary test results would take a week to determine. By that time I'd returned to St. John with a heavy load on my mind. Bob did not take the potential news happily. It wasn't that he was a selfish person. We'd just gotten settled in our new lives and up to this point Bob was carrying more of the everyday load than I was. Our finances were still in disarray, and my job was tenuous. I suggested we head for a beach to sooth our souls.

The quiet solitude of Lamshure Bay gave Bob the backdrop to speak his mind. He didn't like the idea that I would consider major surgery my body didn't require when there was even a small chance that something could go wrong. Bob reminded me that I didn't eat a completely healthy diet and that I was physically out of shape and I had high cholesterol. The ruggedness of St. John hadn't had the time to change my life-style yet and besides, I hated doctors and medications of any kind and had a low tolerance for pain. He feared the worst. I reminded him the first test results weren't even in and it was unlikely I'd pass. Then I pulled the float out from underneath his sunning body and gave him a reassuring kiss underwater to change the mood.

The week passed slowly as I tele-commuted, tried my best to stay focused and did extra chores around the apartment. At work, there were rumors of layoffs in the wind and I felt sure I was to be a part of them. The VP who'd been my biggest supporter in this telecommuting experiment had left the company and so had my group's Director. The acting Director had little use for remote workers unless they were direct revenue producers. And my supervisor was under a lot of pressure. In the evenings instead of working with clay, to relieve the pressure I did research on the Internet on diabetes, kidney donors, and options, while the cats perfected their new skills of ambushing night geckos out on the porch.

The cats were thoroughly enjoying life on St. John, but they were quickly losing a few of their nine lives. Our outdoor explorer ran home one afternoon and into the bedroom with a piece of prickly pear cactus firmly attached to his back. The cactus was almost as big as he was. It took a lot of coaxing to get the wailing baby out from underneath the bed so I could gently disentangle him. Our princess got braver every day in her own explorations. Bob heard her early one evening sliding down the metal roof off our upstairs bedroom porch and caught her just in time before she fell three stories down to the hard surface below. Life was precious.

The social worker with the hospital transplant group tried to put Joe's situation into perspective when she called a week later with the test results.

"Don't let anyone pressure you. This is purely elective surgery. Your kidney donation is not the only alternative," she said. " In fact, it's not a cure, just a temporary solution. It's your decision and you have to do what's right for you, not for anyone else."

Five minutes later we lost power for the rest of the afternoon. Was it a sign from above?

"Your kidney is the only alternative. This is a life or death decision. It's about your brothers life," was the alternative opinion I got from Janine minutes after the fans came back on. Her quality of life was going downhill as quickly as Joe's was. And her frustration over the doctors' unwillingness to accept her as a donor rankled. To her, my personal concerns were trivial.

Initial tests showed that I shared none of the six genes known to show compatibility between donor and recipient. I wasn't surprised.

Joe and I had such differing personalities, I just knew I couldn't have shared compatible genes. However, with today's anti-rejection drugs, this was a minor issue. My blood cells did not attack his when mixed together, which was a more important test. Well, that hardly surprised me at all. My cells were just being overly polite just like my quick offer to risk my life in Paradise to improve my brother's own quality of life.

There were more tests to be done, and I was asked to fly back to Boston only two days later to continue the testing process. I nixed the idea. It was unreasonable to fly to Boston within two days with my tenuous job situation, a husband who was unhappy and little time to adjust to the life decision I faced. Suggesting an alternative, I asked that some of the blood work be done locally on either St. John or St. Thomas. Research showed that requested blood could be taken on either island and shipped overnight to Boston. But, the mainland doctors were partial to their own labs and would only trust those samples and those results.

We were reaching the height of hurricane season. Prepared by buying all the staples recommended by the Red Cross brochures and the local newspapers, we'd begun to think it was all a waste. While we'd had nary a hurricane so far, we did have the occasional tropical wave which was the local lingo for a strong storm front. Each wave brought torrents of rain along with strong winds. Sometimes the rain seemed to be coming from a purely horizontal direction. A small hole from a rotted corner of our kitchen door brought regular pools of water onto our tiled floor and the noise drowned out conversation. While we were grateful for the natural filling of our cistern, each rain shower fell so fast that much water rolled off the roof without making it into the gutter system. It mattered, since the gutters fed the cistern that was the concrete water containment area built beneath our building and was our sole source of water for bathing and cleaning. Only souls living in downtown Cruz Bay had access to the islands public water supply.

My next business trip included a vacation day spent at the hospital and the day after both my arms were covered with bruises from the needle work. I almost didn't get there at all. Hurricane Erika just grazed the Virgin Islands the night before my plane was scheduled to leave St. Thomas. It hit us with minimum force, hardly more than the occasional tropical waves we'd already experienced. By the next morning the rain had stopped when Bob drove me to the ferry dock to catch the early ferry to St. Thomas but the ferry dock was deserted and there wasn't a boat in sight. A half-hour of talking with the few locals milling around led us to the commercial barge dock at the Creek where all the barges and ferries were lashed together as protection from the now distant hurricane. No one knew when any would start running again. Although the water was rough, the sun was peaking through the clouds as we made our way back towards Rendezvous Bay and our apartment.

Two hours later, a phone call to the ferry company confirmed that the first ferry would leave at noon. I was able to change my plane reservations, although I was told the airlines had not cancelled any flights. When I finally arrived at the airport that afternoon and passed through customs, I was greeted by a crowd of tired and annoyed travelers. No planes had left the ground all day despite the telephone claims of the airline, and once through US Customs and Immigration, those people were isolated at the gate area.

The food concession areas were closed due to the hurricane scare and everyone was hungry. Apparently the airport personnel were doing what little they could. An airline ground crew member offered to play Good Samaritan and go down the road to a snack shack to buy food, but he needed cash up front. Many were wary, but their hunger won out as most gave him their orders and their money.

An hour later we boarded the plane to San Juan and the airplane propellers began to turn. The Good Samaritan hadn't arrived back with food and some grumbled and others sighed, while one person made disparaging comments on being robbed on his way out of town. But, most were smiling when the back door suddenly opened to reveal the ground crew hero with bags in both arms and one held under his chin.

He apologized for the delay, explaining it was difficult to find any place open because of the hurricane. As he passed out food, he offered sandwiches and meat pates – ground meat encrusted in a flaky pastry - as an alternative to requested hamburgers. Most people were extremely grateful, but when one person grumbled about a necessary but creative substitution to their request, I felt a strong urge to do bodily harm. The airline worker deserved a medal.

Eventually I made it to the hospital in Boston, taking the tests a day later than planned. Each test was affirmative. I was a surprisingly healthy person, unlikely to get diabetes in the future, and assuming the final tests were positive, a great candidate for kidney donation.

The doctors and my brother Joe were all hoping for an early October operation. I was thinking more like late February. By then, my husband would have a strong local support system and our tenth wedding anniversary and the romantic ski trip we'd planned would be history. Most importantly, I wanted time to live a little of the life we'd found in Paradise. Then I'd be ready to take a risk.

The pressure to make a final decision and commit to a timeframe was strong. Joe's doctor explained the medical reasoning for doing the operations quickly, and it was clear that late February was not a good option for Joe. My own Internet research bore this out. He also said I should not feel pressured to make any decision. Fat chance.

I talked out the issue with my multi-cultured hitchhiking acquaintances. Some thought it was a wonderful gift to give, while others said they wouldn't do it for anyone. It appeared most West Indies natives fell into the latter camp, although everyone seemed to know someone with diabetes. The rumor that I was giving my brother a kidney started around town and soon, even strangers knew. Like a local celebrity, "Make room for the brave kidney lady," was the startling assistance I heard trying to pigeonhole my car near the post office one afternoon. "Yo da ki'nee lady – Go'd be wi'd yo," greeted a hitchhiker I'd never met before. My husband was experiencing similar treatment. He was slowly accepting the inevitable.

I knew it was childish to want to be selfish and self-centered and stay on St. John. If I had to donate a kidney I wanted my parents, my husband or even my friends to take the decision out of my hands and insist I get it over with. But it was my burden to decide my fate. I spent an entire day driving on the back roads of St. John searching for a sign. But there was none. Even the fork in the road sign, now in dire need of a new paint job, yielded no help despite a long hard stare.

Faced with the question, "If the tables were turned, would your brother give you his kidney?" I was sure I knew the answer. I asked him this question directly, and Joe's "I wouldn't be able to with my medical problems" was an unsatisfactory response that solidified his unspoken answer in my mind. Still, if I didn't help my brother, I knew I would have difficulty living with myself. The last test required minor surgery and would need to be done just days before donating the kidney. Deciding if this test was positive I would go through with it, I knew I was doing it all for me and not just for Joe. October it would be, but a week later than everyone hoped. A weight was lifted from my shoulders.

Bob got us free tickets to take a ride on the Atlantis submarine as a thank you for helping out a business acquaintance in St. Thomas. His weekly work hours had become steadier and his client base was continuously growing and his local popularity didn't surprise me any more. The boat trip across the harbor towards Buck Island was relaxing. It was my first time in a submarine of any kind and I had high expectations. While the excursion through coral reefs and marine life was fun, it barely compared with a nice afternoon snorkeling on St. John. But, who could complain?

On the ride home, there were promises made to Bob. Five days in the hospital, ten days to recover nearby and then I'd be home. Bob would go to Boston to see me through the final test results, then leave for home without staying through the kidney surgery, which would only make him a nervous wreck. He'd return two weeks later to bring me home. My sister-in-law had planned to return to her full-time workload as a lawyer a short week after surgery. Published recovery time ranged from four to eight weeks, with most people falling into the latter camp. I wouldn't even try to live up to Janine's superwoman estimate and push the recovery.

I was determined to minimize my family involvement during the ordeal. Birdie had offered to let me recuperate at her home after surgery. It was the perfect solution. I wanted to wallow in my own pain and not be constantly reminded of my "great sacrifice" as my parents were calling it, or the gratefulness of my sister-in-law. Normalcy as soon as possible is what I really wanted, and my best friend would surely cajole me into it.

Bob met me at the hospital in Boston upon completion of that last test as we tried to carve out a weekend together before the big surgery. While waiting for me to be discharged, he walked the halls of the hospital selling raffle tickets for the St. John Volunteer Rescue group to the nursing staff. The Rescue group was hoping to raise money for our first "Jaws of Life" toolkit on St. John. It had become a big priority with the recent influx of enclosed recreation vehicles and the hourly cross-island bus service St John now enjoyed. When only open sided jeeps and open air taxis were the norm, no one worried about extraction equipment. The hospital was a perfect place to share island woes. Within minutes he'd sold all the tickets he'd thought to bring north with him.

Our weekend together was a blur. It was the first time back in New England for Bob but even under different circumstances he'd rather have been on St. John. It was cold and wet and miserable most of the time. I sent Bob home at dawn the day before the kidney surgery so he could prep for a first-aid test and get his mind on pleasanter things.

Birdie took that day off. She decided we both needed a diversion and suggested we travel to Connecticut and spend the day at a gambling casino. We'd spent a day like this once before and had lots of fun. This time it was a bust. Neither of us could stay focused, and after a couple of hours we gave it up. We were both subdued the entire way to Boston where I'd stay overnight until my 5AM check-in at the hospital. I was glad when she left, as I needed to face my fears alone.

The surgery went fine for both Joe and I. Amazingly, I got to know my oldest brother better in those few days in the hospital ward than I had in my forty some odd years on this planet. With a seven year age difference we'd just never been very close. He didn't understand why I'd moved to Paradise and I didn't understand why he didn't follow his dreams. In the end, it was our common paranoia and then misery that united us.

My brother insisted on morphine to ease his pain, then other prescription drugs to continue the dulling process. I was more afraid of side effects than anything else, and opted for an epidural short term and then simple Tylenol hoping I'd recover faster if I wasn't doped up. I wanted no Tylenol-3 or Tylonol-2 but just simple basic Tylenol. Joe complained that I was trying to be a martyr, but I retorted that I was being cautious, fearing that any side effect might keep me in the hospital longer than necessary.

It wasn't that the pain was unbearable three days after surgery, but I knew it would be bad soon. When I wanted another dose of Tylenol one hour before the prescribed six-hour interval had passed, the nurses acted like I was a drug addict. Stopping by my brother's room on the slow shuffle back to mine, I whined and told Joe it was unfair. His spirits were high, just as he was from all the drugs, and he found the situation humorous. I threw a pillow at him and left Joe laughing as he took his fine Percocet. Ten minutes later, I was unsuccessfully trying to get comfortable in my bed again, when I heard a loud commotion in the hallway.

"I don't care if it's just aspirin, you cannot just take drugs from the drug cart. Your sister will have to wait another half-hour. Now get away from there." Shuffling preceded Joe's shy entrance to my bedside. "I tried," he said with a grin. Wow, my brother tried to steal drugs for me! I loved this man.

I was out of the hospital in five days and was determined to return home on schedule. Bob called almost daily to cheer me up with news from Paradise. He sent a homemade get-well card with a photograph of my favorite rocking chair on our porch, overlooking the gardens and St. Thomas in the distance. Inside, the card told me that my husband and even the cats were proud of me and missed me and were waiting anxiously for me to come home and watch the sunsets with them. It was the sweetest thing.

Birdie opened her home to me, and made sure I had food to eat and things to read. But, she didn't overly pamper me. By the third day, I only hurt when I laughed which unfortunately was often. Every evening we traded adventures from the summer months and I brought her up to date on everything happening on St. John. I had plenty of time to paint gold "St. John, USVI" inscriptions to the hundred-odd medallions I'd brought North and worry about how I'd find time to get the other hundred completed for my first commission's deadline.

Joe recovered faster than I did. The volume of medications that would be his future depressed him, but his personality was back and I was glad. I was embarrassed that I had been so afraid to give him a kidney and that I'd considered a few months disruption in my life to be such a big deal. On the phone every day we compared recovery pains and I was disappointed when he felt better than I did.

My mission to get home two weeks after surgery was accomplished on time thanks to Bob's playing 'Sherpa from the Himalayas' and carrying my entire luggage. A plump pillow provided added padding for my side. The doctors had insisted that I lift no more than five pounds for a couple of weeks, and then not lift any significant weight for a solid eight weeks. Even the taxi driver on St. Thomas was extra kind as he tried hard to avoid the numerous potholes and minimize the jolting. As he avoided each one, the driver turned to me with a grin and asked if I was okay. I made Bob give him an extra big tip.

At home, our neighbor Jay, who'd volunteered to cat-sit for a few days, also had a warm meal waiting on the kitchen counter for our arrival. It was just what we both needed. The next morning, an orchid plant that smelled like chocolate arrived as a welcome home present from the St.

John Rescue folks and five people called to welcome me back. I was humbled and felt undeserved of all the attention. What had seemed like a horrible life decision a month ago now seemed trivial. I was happy and home and my brother now had a brighter future. And in two more months I'd have everything behind me while Joe would have a lifetime of adjustments and medications ahead of him.

I still had one more challenge ahead. My workplace was having its yearly kickoff meeting the first week of November. It was only one week after my return to St. John. Yes, I made it. But not without a plump pillow by my side and not without second thoughts. Bob grumbled, but I promised to make porters carry my bags and travel as light as possible. The trip was worth it. While I was uncomfortable part of every day, I was being productive again. But, upon my return to St. John five days later, I was ready to stay put for a while.

In fact, I was in a panic. I still had eighty medallions to make for my first commission and a host of other craft items were needed to fill even a tiny booth during St. John Saturday. If I put off the November event, I knew it would be a long time before I got around to doing it again. Raw materials were strewn everywhere in the living room and kitchen, and I worked feverishly. Even waiting for that 800 number connection to the mainland when trying to reach my company's computer system gave me the two minutes necessary to accomplish some small task. Meanwhile, my recovery continued at an accelerated pace.

The worst part of my recovery was my surgeon's insistence that I stay out of the pool and the ocean. When the doctor first told me I must refrain from taking a dip in the swimming pool for six to eight weeks after surgery, I balked. The surgeon had just finished telling me that I could resume normal showers a short week after surgery. He'd lived his life in Boston, and it showed.

It took all of my patience to explain to this urban doctor that I lived on a little island where water is scarce. "A short dip in the swimming pool followed by a navy shower with as little water as possible is our daily norm," I complained. "And, my regular dip in the pool is the least strenuous part of the chore."

But the surgeon was hard to convince. I tried a new tact, asking why he didn't want me in the pool. "You'll strain yourself and won't be able to resist the urge to swim," he said.

"Our pool is tiny. Besides, I'm not a tourist. I'm very happy to spend just five or ten minutes floating," I persisted.

Finally he acquiesced. "Five minutes max, after four weeks. And only the pool. Ten minutes, in six weeks. No ocean for at least eight weeks so you won't be tempted to strain yourself. And you must immediately dry off afterwards and keep the scar tissue out of the sun."

I barely survived the weeks without a dip in the pool. While I was careful and immediately changed to dry clothes, my sea baths started two weeks earlier than the doctor ordered. It just wasn't worth a phone call to Boston to convince him I could be lazy in the water.

St. John Trivia

June is Hurricane Preparedness Month in the USVI. Most take the hurricane season seriously, stocking up on water, canned goods, plastic tarps, and prescription medicines.

Many St. Johnians are addicted to the Weather Channel on Cable TV, especially during hurricane season. Local newspapers publish hurricane-tracking maps early in the season, showing longitude and latitude coordinates for each island in the Caribbean. Tracking the storms from the time they form off the east coast of Africa is a favorite local pastime.

Hurricane season in the USVI lasts from June until November, with the greatest likelihood of storms occurring in September and early October.

Chapter Eleven
Every Day is a Holiday

Bob and I had much to be thankful for, so this first year on-island we wanted a Thanksgiving we'd remember forever. Two years earlier we passed the holiday on St. John with a traditional feast at a waterside restaurant in the heart of downtown Cruz Bay. This time a restaurant just wouldn't cut it. I pondered alternatives as I readied for my first postsurgical dip in the pool on a hot November afternoon.

"Unbelievable" was not the word that came out of my mouth, but it sums up the sight that faced me from our porch. A mysterious green algae had grown overnight in our pool and it looked very ominous. It could not deter me from my goal – my first postsurgical dip. Down the spiral staircase, I took a left turn instead of the usual right towards our pool. Across the trellised bougainvillea and down another flight of stairs I came face to face with my neighbor's pool, clean and inviting. Thank goodness, Moe and Bev had built two pools on the property, one for each nearly identical building. The lower pool was slightly longer and narrower than our own, but suited my purpose just fine.

My neighbor Jay sat in a corner soaking up the sunrays. Her closed eyes were betrayed by her grin as she taunted "Go to your own pool, lady," while contrarily patting the chair next to hers in invitation. Jay was always philosophical and creative when she was relaxed, so I posed my Thanksgiving dilemma and hoped for the best. I wasn't disappointed.

"Wouldn't it be fun," she asked, "to invite everyone who lives here to share in a Thanksgiving pot luck dinner at the pool?"

"Have you seen my pool?" I countered.

"Yuck. But the odds are good that at least one of the pools will be in okay condition. Besides, with enough food and drinks, it won't matter. Andre can cook a big ham for the occasion."

"And I'll roast a turkey," I offered without thinking.

On a roll, Jay suggested we could invite, not only everyone who lived nearby, but also some people we knew who'd only moved here recently. And then there were the few boat people we'd both become friendly with, for whom cooking a turkey dinner was nearly impossible. Everyone would be asked to contribute some food or paperware item.

The men would round up tables and chairs and tarps for shade, and I would only have to make a turkey. In my oven from hell, I realized moments later when the warm pool water finally soaked through my brain. Our stove was a small gas one, with barely room for four burners on top. It was like those in the other two bedroom apartments, with a big distinction. My stove knobs had no writing on them. I'd laughed at first, until my guessing resulted in a couple of inedible meals. I'd visited Bev to make a paper template of her own stove knobs, and wrote the appropriate markings onto my knobs with permanent ink. Another failed meal brought me knocking at Jay's door to make a template from a stove identical to mine. It still didn't matter. My oven really needed only two settings. "On" and "Burned". Still, I looked forward to the turkey challenge to prove I was smarter than my tiny hellhole of an oven. It would be a unique Thanksgiving.

Although it wasn't yet Thanksgiving, I was already anxious to unpack all the Holiday goods which were in the last of the unopened *Paradise Expedition* boxes. But, knee-high in packing materials, I realized I had less desire to decorate than I thought. Our apartment was finally beginning to have a live-in feel to it and the thought of over-decorating for the holidays depressed me. On the other hand, I did want some Christmas and Hanukah trivia and I hoped to get Bob to cut down a local version of the fresh cut Christmas tree.

Jay was in an opposite quandary. Ted, who lived below her apartment, had given her a twenty-foot long Century plant he'd cut for a traditional island Christmas tree before deciding it was too big to be useful. With her cathedral ceiling, the tree made a perfect focal point for the living room. But, she lamented, most of her Christmas decorations were stuck in Rhode Island due to a family squabble and her house would be abnormally bare for the holiday season. Another neighborly chat with Jay, this time at my newly cleaned pool, solved both our dilemmas.

"I have more decorations than one person on St. John should be allowed to have. I'd be thrilled if you'd take some to use in your apartment." All were unpacked and needed organizing anyway, but I could see the doubt on her face.

"You don't need to worry about any getting destroyed, as we expect that during the holidays. There are enough decorations to do justice to your tree with enough left over for the smaller one I hope to have. Really…" I added for emphasis.

"Only if we have a holiday party at our place to show it all off," Jay compromised. "And Andre and I will take care of everything. We'll celebrate Hanukkah and Christmas and whatever and invite all the neighbors and our friends."

Better her place than mine, I thought. It was perfect. My apartment would stay rather clean and we'd get a party out of the deal. Christmas was well under control before Thanksgiving even arrived. Besides, I had other things on my mind.

Bob had signed me up for booth space at the next St. John Saturday event, which was to be held two short days after Thanksgiving. I needed more goods to sell and I needed them fast. Enlisting Jay and her daughter Jessie, we made little princess crowns made of foil and ribbons that were sure to be a big hit with the kids. I made doorknob hangers like the "Do Not Disturb" signs found in hotel rooms, with island scenes I designed on my computer. Birdie helped us from New

Hampshire, by critiquing the designs I e-mailed her via the Internet. Even Bob got into the spirit of things and laminated and trimmed these unique items. He borrowed a couple of doorknobs from friends in town that he mounted on a board as a display rack.

Digging into my craft supplies, I came up with a large batch of earrings with a Christmas theme that Birdie had delivered to my garage a year earlier. With sudden inspiration Jessie and I gathered seashells and spray painted them gold. We tied them in mesh bags, added a blue ribbon to each, and tagged them as Island Hanukah Geld. Attached to each ribbon was a short explanation of how pirates in the Caribbean had stolen all the local gold, and so true to St. John's unique style we offered this new version of the traditional holiday gift. It was silly, but so were we. Thanksgiving was two days away and I'd forgotten to buy a turkey.

By noon on Thanksgiving Day, I'd been hovering over my temperamental oven for hours and I was tired. Just that morning Bob told me he thought we were about to run out of propane gas for the stove. We hadn't filled it for six months and the gas company was closed for the holiday. I prayed the gas would last until the turkey was cooked. Maybe being low on gas helped. Or maybe it was constantly opening the oven to make sure the broiler hadn't suddenly turned itself on. By some strange miracle, the turkey came out plump, juicy and unscorched.

The party was a lively one. There was enough food for an army. An open tent provided shade for the food, and a motley combination of lawn furniture was spread throughout the garden. Lots of people showed up and some sat on the edge of the pool while being occasionally splashed by the younger set. There was music for every taste and the good times flowed freely. So did the spiked cups of Jell-O that never seemed to run out. Andre's ham was a hit, which was a good thing. He'd mistakenly chosen a spiral cut style at a St. Thomas supermarket, which ended up costing a full day's pay. Everyone insisted it had been worth his pain.

The only low point in the festivities was discovering the army of fire ants that lived near the pool. It was hard to believe such tiny creatures could cause such excruciating pain. The second they found exposed flesh they bit with all their might. But, even they couldn't spoil the fun for long. By nightfall exhaustion overtook our fun. Bob and I went home, determined to call it a night. But, we were drawn back by the laughter from the lingering crowd below. Again and again we were drawn downstairs to join the last of the party die-hards taking dips in the pool and philosophizing in the darkness.

The urge for an island Christmas tree set off an idea in my mind to solve another problem. The day after Thanksgiving, I insisted to Bob that the cutting had to be done immediately. Bob was caught off guard and still in a festive mood from the day before. He'd gotten tools and gloves together before he remembered he was supposed to be grouchy. By then it was too late to back out. He stalked down the dusty road. I followed in high spirits, thinking some things never changed.

A traditional St. John Christmas tree meant, for some, the dead stalk from a Century plant and the gem Bob chose was growing a mere two hundred yards above our apartment on a hill, but getting to it required a gingerly hike through the bush. The stalk was also twisted and slanted and not overly attractive while only fifty yards further up the slope was the tree of my dreams. I begged and I pleaded and I sang Christmas carols while pointing to the tree I wanted. Bob turned a deaf ear and began sawing away at its twisted sister.

Surprisingly, though the Century plant was extremely strong and hard, it weighed very little. I was able to carry my end of our fifteen foot tree with just three fingers which was a relief since I was under doctors orders to carry little weight. Bob and I walked down past a beautiful late blooming Century plant that had been tempting on our walk up the steep hill. But we'd resisted since we'd both heard horror tales from people who'd cut down a fresh stalk. That beauty wasn't worth the oozing sap that would follow a few days later. It was a great way to ruin anything on or under the tree.

We startled some tourists coming up a switchback and they almost stalled their car on the steep road as they slowed down to stare at our strange lumberjack antics. Back at the apartment, Bob cut off the bottom of the long stalk and placed the remaining eight-foot high island Christmas tree top into our patiently waiting tree stand. I had been vindicated in mailing it to St. John. Still, there would be no need to water this 'fresh' Christmas tree.

I put the bottom part of the stalk into a large bucket, which we then filled with stones. Bob was directed to cut back its branches of seedpods to bare branches a mere eight inches out from the central stalk. Instantly I had the display stand I'd been searching for to hang the foil fairy crowns for the St. John Saturday crafts fair. It was crooked, but it worked. Bob fumed.

"You tricked me into doing two chores today, when I only promised to do one." Holiday season chores always seemed to bring out the child in my husband in good ways and in bad ones.

"Rather painlessly," I dryly commented. St. John Saturday was twelve hours away.

The craft items were a big hit the next day. Jay and Jessie both came down to help set up. Bob graciously helped to unload the car, knowing he'd have hours at the beach without interruptions that day. Conscious of my recent surgery, the assistance was welcome. While Jay had to go back to work for most of the day, Jessie stayed and found a friend to help out and keep her company at the same time. Steel band music from the bandstand in the park set a festive mood that day. My fellow vendors were pleasant and the holiday spirit was everywhere. Bob's desertion was quickly forgotten.

Our neighbors, Ted and Katie, were selling Christmas wreaths made from the seedpod laden Century plant branches. It was recycling at it's best. Ted had been making a few dollars on the side cutting down traditional island Christmas trees for seasonal residents who didn't want to walk through the bush this year. The wreaths were the by-products of cutting the trees down to size, since branches can extend over twenty-five feet down the length of the tree. For added variety, Katie had made some beautiful wreaths threading together the empty seedpods of the ever-abundant tan-tan trees that sprout up on roadsides everywhere. Their booth was a big hit and was photographed for posterity, appearing in the next *Tradewinds* newspaper.

In between customers I started dancing along with the Mocko Jumbies that provided entertainment for the tourists. These Mocko Jumbies were costumed dancers on eight-foot high stilts. Imagine my surprise when I realized one directly above me was another talented neighbor who'd moved here two years earlier. As each ferry arrived with more visitors from St. Thomas, the Mocko Jumbies moved to the docks to provide a special welcome and direct them back towards the park. I did my part by offering to take photographs of tourists and Jumbies with the tourists' cameras as they passed by.

Meanwhile, my own sales were respectable. The youngsters helping in my booth were a boon, especially when a short sun shower threatened to ruin my goods. As is typical, the first drop of rain signaled a downpour to follow mere seconds later. Quickly we whipped out plastic to cover everything but ourselves, knowing the shower would be over in jut a few minutes. The sun stayed shining throughout.

Along with a free lunch chosen from a nearby food vendor, I rewarded my little helpers with their choice of souvenirs from my own booth. One selected a necklace and the other a key chain, both made from polymer clay. The day wound down as the sun was setting. Bob returned and packed the car without complaint and took credit for being a good husband. He'd found a beach he'd shared only with the birds and the sea life to while away the hours, but I think I had more fun that day.

The next day we both spent a quiet day at Jumbie beach on the north shore with no responsibilities and no intrusions. Somehow, even the boats knew to stay away from the little cove that day. I took my first sea-bath in months, two weeks earlier than the doctor had ordered.

It was heaven. Palm and sea-grape trees provided shade, our picnic basket yielded delectable grazing, and a good book helped pass the time while Bob sunned himself on his snow float. There was no place I wanted to be more than St. John that weekend. It wasn't even December and yet the holidays were now in full gear.

The little gifts I gave my crafts fair volunteers were a big hit in the schoolyard the next day. The whole sixth grade class begged my young friends to find them some they could buy. After school, Jessie came knocking on my door, interrupting a business conference call and asked if she could bring a selection of clay trinkets to school for her friends to choose from. After a few minutes of patience which seemed like years to my eleven year old friend, Jessie left with an eclectic selection and the promise of a finders fee she could use towards her own holiday spending. It was another strange success as an artisan.

Jessie personally asked me to attend her small school's Christmas pageant. Along with the invitation came an admonition to wear 'real shoes and a dress too'. This child had always seen me in sandals or barefoot and the only dresses she'd seen me wear were the flowery floor length shifts I'd come to prefer over shorts and a T-shirt for comfort's sake. The night of the event I went all out and wore an outfit more suited to a formal summer's concert in Boston. I wore high heels and added makeup and jewelry to complete the attire. Jessie hardly recognized me and even her mother couldn't stop staring.

The pageant was great fun, starting with darling pre-schoolers in their angel garb and seasonal songs in both Spanish and English. My favorite was their rendition of the Twelve Days of Christmas, with a decidedly island twist. "Nine Harried Tourists... Four Swaying Palms... And a Donkey Braying in a Hog's Plum Tree" made me laugh so hard I almost fell on the floor with the three-year-olds.

Exactly eight weeks after surgery, the time specified for my official recovery, I was confronted with an unplanned business trip to California. It was mid-December and the trip might bring an opportunity to find a few last minute gifts for Bob. Convinced I'd babied myself enough, I decided to carry along my notebook computer so I could keep up with my normal workload in between meetings. The travel between the USVI and the West Coast of the US was long and tiring. I learned new respect and sensitivity for the tourists who make the long trek to visit our islands for their vacation.

By the time the return flight disembarked on St. Thomas, my side was aching from the weight of the bag I carried. My computer couldn't be checked as luggage like the rest of my load. Besides, the welcome basket of goodies that had greeted me at my hotel from a company in San Jose was filled with local delicacies too fragile to pack. Minutes after arriving home, with relaxing my sole goal, Bob reminded me that it was Friday night and we had two parties to attend. He was ready to celebrate, since that very day he'd been offered full fledged employment with Bestech, along with the illusionary benefits and security that came with no longer being a mere contractor. Reminded that no business trips were scheduled for the next seven weeks and the holidays were upon us, I got my second wind and within minutes was ready to party.

I sat in the passenger seat of my own Geo Tracker as Bob began the slow roll down the switchback towards town. The seat was at an angle with the backrest reclined, which is my husband's preferred riding position. I didn't bother to make it more upright before reaching for the seatbelt to secure myself in. As my right arm, buckle in hand, reached across to find the buckle latch, a sharp pain jolted my body. I screamed. Bob braked the car, and though he was driving at a snail's pace, it was by the barest of margins that my head missed the windshield.

Just as suddenly as it started, the pain was gone. I tried again with the seat buckle only to reach the same painful conclusion. Perhaps the notebook computer I'd traveled with was too heavy. Regardless, after eight weeks of babying myself, instead of a full recovery, I'd pulled the slowly healing inside stitches at the back end of my scar line. For months, with slowly lessening pain, I'd pull them again and feel the urge to call my brother to see how he was holding up. The scar tissue was permanent. I rode illegally through Cruz Bay that night without a seatbelt and didn't care.

Our two parties that evening were marked with the diversity that had become our lives. First was the annual Holiday party at the local sail-making business where the crowded fun was already underway. The insides of the warehouse style workspace had been lined with fresh palm fronds and Christmas lights to create a festive atmosphere. A sea of food and beverage selections was being enjoyed by many while others danced to the stereo music or chatted away in clusters. The water cooler that had been turned into a margarita dispenser was my first stop. Within minutes my pains were forgotten. Bob and I mingled comfortably with the eclectic crowd, some in cut-off jeans and others in pressed slacks or dresses. Too soon, someone asking me the time on my watch squashed our fun. We were overdue at our other engagement of the evening.

The large vacation resort near our home was our next destination. While we knew it would be an upscale dinner dance, we were unprepared for the formality of the occasion. Beaded gowns and, yes, even tuxedos adorned the outdoors gala event. There were no sandals at this party, and the only shorts were those paired with crisp blazers and ties. Each place setting at the sit-down dinner tables included a party favor. These were extravagant seasonal ornaments discreetly marked with the initials SJYC and the year for a take-home keepsake. A live band performed while Bob and I danced under the moonlight. I drank enough that I remember no more pain that night.

Our neighbors had no experience with Hanukah. Bob sought to change that, inviting guests to participate in the lighting of the Menorah each night and sharing the history and traditions of the holiday with all. Some traditions he made up as he went along, but everyone had fun and the sense of community we all felt made me keep quiet. I'd lined our porch with miniature Christmas lights and discovered my downstairs neighbors, Ricky and Karen, always lined the pool area and gardens with lights too. A large electric Menorah crowned our upper porch for all in the valley to see.

You couldn't see much from the road, but at night our back yard was an enchanted space that made me smile all month long. Every tree and bush was covered with lights, each with it's own distinctive color, creating a nighttime rainbow of delight. Inside, our Century Plant tree tilted somewhat no matter how Bob tried to turn it. Even with lights, and decorations, and tinsel it reminded me of a Charlie Brown Christmas tree. But when we turned out the living room lamps it was spectacular. With the glittering porch and garden below as a backdrop it was the most beautiful tree we'd ever had.

Jay remembered to include Hanukah decorations in her apartment for her promised holiday party, which pleased Bob tremendously. It seemed that a good portion of the island managed to stop by and spread good cheer. There was no dancing at Jay's party, but the long day and night of good food and plentiful drinks and lively conversation interspersed with dips in the pool left little room for much more.

A week later I was searching for a different kind of party as I danced between the docks in Cruz Bay on the morning of Christmas Eve. I was not a happy camper.

My husband's older sister, Eve, and her family were scheduled to visit us, just for the day. They were on a Caribbean cruise and the ship would dock in St. Thomas, only five miles away. Bob and I had been psyched for their visit. However, these fine folks had forgotten to tell us what ship they'd be on, and by the time Bob called them to ask, they were on their way. The local newspaper told us there would be seven ships in port on Christmas Eve! On the designated day, Bob headed to work convinced they wouldn't show up and telling me to call him if they ever did. Bah Humbug. I drove down to the barge dock in the early morning, hoping they'd arrive soon.

It was my first real experience with the cruise ship excursion routines. The barge dock where most cruise ship passengers disembark is in Cruz Bay Creek, which is out of sight from the regular ferry dock. I'd noticed cruise ship crowds many times when driving past, but I didn't appreciate the magnitude of the operation. It was like a well oiled machine, with employees from the cruise ships, the ferries, the tour companies and the taxis all working in concert with each other.

With arms waving in patterns as though they were directing aircraft, workers chanted and pointed "Annaberg over here, Trunk Bay over here, Island Tours over here". Continuous masses of tourists poured off ferryboats lined up next to the barges and followed directions like they were used to the routine. There were, of course, a few strays, but they were quickly intercepted and directed to the correct waiting lines. It was amazing.

Bob's relatives were not there. As the empty boats departed, so did I. I rushed to the Ferry dock where the hourly ferry was coming in. There were no relatives on the regular ferry from Red Hook, but seeing a coming ferry boat divert towards the Creek, I returned to my earlier location knowing more cruise ship passengers were arriving over there. I repeated this dance throughout the morning, finally giving up. The phone rang just as I walked into the apartment, saddened and exhausted. It was my brother-in-law's secretary on the phone from Massachusetts. The family would be landing at the regular ferry dock in five minutes. Town was at least ten minutes away.

Twelve minutes later, I'd phoned my husband, parked my car on the dock and was kissing and hugging Eve and the other long lost relatives. After dodging tourists driving on the wrong side of the road and waiting patiently for a water truck to ascend Jacobs Ladder, an atrocious hill on the outskirts of town, our caravan of two cars got everyone to our home. Smiling. It was Christmas Eve. Bob's relatives had exactly two hours before they had to take a return ferry back to Charlotte Amalie, as their cruise ship was docked at the Sub-Base rather than the normal Havensight location where most ships arrived. The Sub-Base meant an even longer trip back.

That two hours was a blur. Bob quickly made sandwiches for the hungry teenagers, while I gave their parents a penny tour of our apartment. Then we all got back into the vehicles for a whirlwind tour of St. John. Up over Gift Hill we took them, as they hung on for dear life. We made a quick stop at the ruins at Catherineburg where I told them about, but didn't have time to show them, my favorite windmill site with its tunnels and gravity fed molasses storage pits. A roadside overlook showing islands in BVI over the north shore was our next stop. Onto Bordeaux Mountain we took them where they marveled at the view of Coral Bay.

Unfortunately, we were too paranoid about their time constraints to drive them back to town via the slower north shore route through the National Park. Instead we took them back down Centerline road while entertaining them with stories about cows and donkeys and goats. And then they were gone. It was hard to believe they'd been here at all. That evening, I looked out at the glittering lights of cruise ships settled off shore for the night, and wished them all a merry Christmas.

While Bob and I spent Christmas day quietly together, Christmas didn't end the festivities for us. There were still Kwanza and New Years Eve and Three Kings Day, celebrated with great importance and parades and pageants. Everyday seemed to bring another holiday. Before we came up for air the second week of January, I was partied out.

St. John Trivia

The three-story police station in Cruz Bay boasts the island's first and only working elevator. After the ribbon-cutting ceremony in 1998 to officially open the building, some of St. John's leading citizens took advantage of the Open House to enjoy their first elevator ride.

St. John's first bona-fide criminal got a free ride a few months later.

Chapter Twelve
Everyone Needs a Vacation

In the middle of high tourist season on St John, our first overnight guests flocked from the continent for a ten-night stay. Unfortunately, we were also in the middle of a drought. Navy showers, using as little water as possible and turning off the water while sudsing up were routine. It wasn't so much the cost to buy a truckload of water to fill our cistern that worried us, but we didn't want to face the wrath of the neighbors who had to chip in for each meager truckload. Bob and I were quietly paranoid about having extra bodies using the cistern. Still, the guestroom was cleaned up and readied. As a special touch, the Century plant display rack from our St. John Saturday fun was painted and recycled into an eccentric hat stand in the corner. Bob caved in and bought a round plastic patio table on St. Thomas that could easily seat four people on the porch for dinner via our still strung Christmas lights and our table candles.

I'd offered use of my Tracker for day trips to our vacationing guests, since my home office often meant days with the vehicle sitting idle. Bob grumbled that it wasn't worth it, especially when I took the barge to St. Thomas to replace worn brakes in anticipation of the visits. Still, I caught Bob cleaning his own car and prepping the back seat for added guests just before the first ones arrived. He complained but he was ready for visitors.

First came my sister-in-law, Dee, from New York City with her long-time girlfriend, Shelly, from upstate New York. Dee had been to St. John with us on our family vacation two years earlier. She knew that St. John wasn't truly the end of the world, and we expected her to show up with just a small carry-on bag for luggage. Instead, when Dee de-embarked from the ferry, it was with two huge suitcases along with the predictable large carry-one bag for each of them. My little Geo Tracker was so overloaded it had a hard time making it to the top of famed Jacobs Ladder even though it hadn't rained for days. If that road had been wet, we never would have made the hill. I brushed aside their comment that they'd brought some food stuffs for us, and just shook my head laughing at how two people could arrive so over-packed for a place where a T-shirt, shorts, and a bathing suit was all it took.

Imagine my surprise when the first large suitcase was opened and I discovered wall to wall food and household items. The next suitcase surprised us all. It too had been filled with foodstuffs, but the sugar and the cornstarch and the flour had burst out of their packaging causing a cloud of white to rush out at us when the cover was opened. It was a disaster. Even more amazing was the sheer quantity and variety of food items that Dee and Shelly had purchased. Even if Bob and I hadn't bought any food since we'd arrived on island, we'd now have a well-stocked pantry. They left nothing out. Finding room for it all took creativity; it took months to eat our way through most of the foodstuffs.

Dee and Shelly were dream guests. They not only brought us a huge supply of foods, but they also cleaned and cooked and accommodated our every whim. The first day was an overcast one, but it gave me an excuse to sneak a day off from work and play tour guide. I showed them all around St. John, pointing out the usual sites interspersed with trivia like the cotton plants growing wild on the other side of Bordeaux Mountain that had been planted by slaves in the eighteen hundreds. After some pushing, Dee took the wheel and got the hang of driving on the left. I started her out on the north shore near Annaberg, where there was little traffic. To her credit, she only wandered to the right side one panicked time. For the rest of the week, they'd be on their own.

Every day was an adventure for the girls, and Bob and I tried not to cringe at their tales each night. They took a wrong turn heading out of town and were nearly to Coral Bay before realizing their mistake and guessing how to get back to our apartment via a relatively direct route in the dark. They explored areas I couldn't bring myself to take my poor vulnerable car. But at least our water shortage fears were unfounded. The girls showered sometimes at Trunk Bay or the Cinnamon Bay campground after their beach time and both were out and about for most waking hours. Except when Shelly insisted on cooking for us. And when Dee decided to stick around one morning to clean the apartment from top to bottom, including the porch. We were truly sorry when they had to return to the States.

I left town the same day they did but at least I'd be back in a few days. On the last day of business in Atlanta, anxious to get back home to the USVI and away from the cold weather that seemed everywhere on the mainland, I discovered what a small world it is. The next day was my sister-in-law Janine's birthday and I called her local florist in New Hampshire for a quick gift. When I gave my billing address, I expected the usual surprised exclamation when I said "USVI" as an answer for the state I lived in. Instead, I got an unusual "Sure, I understand".

The owner of the flower shop was on St. John at that very moment, I was told. He'd be here for another six weeks, as was his custom every winter. I asked where he was staying, and to my surprise, the address was right down the road. Everyone who worked at the flower shop had been to St. John for a vacation in the past year. When asked where we lived on St. John and I replied, "Century Hill" since street addresses mean nothing on this island.

"Oh, you can probably see his roof in Chocolate Hole from there. Say hi to the Boss for us." The florist was still on St. John when our next vacationers from New Hampshire arrived. But first, Bob and I took our own vacation.

Our tenth anniversary was the excuse. We'd planned to spend some days cross-country skiing in Vermont, as we'd done for part of our honeymoon. In fact, our very first date was spent on cross-country ski trail with my future husband trying his best not to laugh as he attempted to teach me the sport. The rest of our anniversary trip would be spent visiting friends, shopping and getting health checkups. Two weeks before the trip, Bob began to balk. He'd adjusted so well to St. John that the idea of cold weather had tarnished his desires.

It was a call from Janine that reaffirmed our plans. Joe would turn fifty on our anniversary date. His wife was planning a surprise birthday party while we were scheduled to be up north, and conveniently the day before our ski resort reservations in Vermont. It was to be a big event that she hoped would raise Joe's spirits and help him forget his medical problems for a few hours. We couldn't refuse.

It was the first time we'd left our cats alone for more than three days since we'd moved to Paradise. We were very concerned about them being cooped up for a whole week with only relative strangers to care for them. Jessie, our eleven-year-old neighbor, chaperoned by her mom Jay, volunteered for the task. Since she had a cat of her own and her mom to ensure regular feedings, we left our babies in her care.

For our first night up north, we stayed with Dan who was now sharing a home he'd bought with Jo, the lady who'd survived the West River camping weekend with him in the ice and snow only the spring before. It was only fair. They'd be visiting us on St. John a few weeks later and like many first time visitors they were anxious to discuss their plans. Bob tried to explain that the timing of getting from the plane to the ferry would depend on the concept of island-time. They couldn't grasp our lack of concern over which ferry they'd be on.

The next day was hectic. Early in the morning we drove past the home of one of my co-workers to drop off my notebook computer for a long needed upgrade during the vacation week. Then we stopped by Birdie's condo to have coffee and pick up some party items for Joe's surprise event that she'd kindly prepared for me. Afterwards, it was on to my mother's house to visit with a brother and his wife who'd flown in from Pittsburgh for the surprise party that evening.

Bob was tasked with the chore of spending the afternoon with Joe under the guise of working on his home computer to keep him occupied and then to get my eternally late brother to the surprise party on time. Meanwhile, I was frantically running around town to buy and then to the rented hall to set up the party decorations instead of clothes shopping with his wife, as my big brother had been led to believe. St. John was a blurry memory.

By six thirty, everything was ready. Over seventy people were gathered in the rented hall including the friends I'd visited with that morning. All were chatting freely and enjoying the poster sized tongue in cheek collages of fifty years in the life of my older brother. The DJ was warming up and the hors d'oeuvres were flowing nicely. My niece, wanting to know everything about St. John that she missed during her two hour Christmas tour was on the lookout with me for my brother Joe at the other side of the huge restaurant complex. Joe expected to find his wife and I waiting there for a quiet dinner foursome with Bob.

The moment I spied Bob and Joe leave their car, I sent my excited niece through the restaurant to the adjoining rental hall to spread the word. I slowly guided the men through the restaurant to the closed door that separated the restaurant from the rented hall. It was only when I stood back and suggested that Joe lead the way that he got suspicious. Before Joe could react, I pushed the door open ahead of him and a rousing Happy Birthday greeted his stare.

The party was more fun than I thought possible. There was a trivia contest on the life and times of my brother, and strange dance contests to boot. Friends and family I hadn't seen in years were all there. While it was my brother's night, it was a sort of pre-anniversary party for my husband and I too. By the time we reached my brothers home late that night for a short nights sleep I was exhausted.

Early the next morning Bob and I departed for three days of skiing in Stowe, Vermont. The day was perfect for a long drive, with the sun shining on freshly snow covered trees while the roads were dry and held little traffic. The inn at Stowe was as fabulous as always. Late afternoon tea and cake followed by a Jacuzzi bubble bath and a quiet supper of Mullagatawny soup and wine in front of a fireplace brought a fine end to the day. It was the antithesis of our life in the islands.

Trail conditions on that first day of cross-country skiing were perhaps the best we'd ever encountered. True to tradition, my husband skied with me for the first twenty minutes, and then he rushed off to the farthest reaches of the trail system while I enjoyed a slower pace absorbing the quiet nature around me. We were on the Von Trapp Family trail system, which was famous for the family that founded it and the pristine variety it offered the day-tripper. By early afternoon, we were tired and traveled to town to do some shopping for local gourmet goodies for our friends back on St. John.

The next two days flew by fast. One evening Bob and I went to the local movie theatre. When we tried to remember the last time we'd done so, I were surprised to realize it had been a full year earlier on our last visit to Vermont. There was no movie theatre on St. John, and the practicalities of going to St. Thomas to get to a theatre always seemed too daunting. Too soon, we had to leave.

My mom was scheduled to have back surgery that day and I wanted to be back in New Hampshire and near the family. My mother's surgery went well, and my brother from Pittsburgh was ensconced in my parents' home to keep a watchful eye on my elderly father. By late evening, Bob and I were at Dan and Jo's home where we'd encamped five nights earlier. It would be our home too for next two days while we stayed in the area to keep doctors' appointments and stock up on household goods that couldn't be gotten in the islands.

On that last day before returning to St. John, we said our good-byes, picked up my newly upgraded computer, dropped off a thank you bouquet of flowers to Birdie, visited my mom in the hospital, and then said good-bye to my dad and brothers. Bob and I were then off to Massachusetts and yet another one night visit with some island enthusiasts. After a fine send-off dinner and good conversation, we were just settling in for the night when my husband suggested I call St. John to check in with Andre and Jay and especially Jessie, who was taking care of our cats. The man of the household answered our call.

"It's about time you called," said my anxious neighbor. "We tried tracking you down for the past twenty-four hours but you were no-where to be found."

I was sure there was an emergency of some kind. "Sorry, Andre, but we weren't sure where we'd be yesterday until just the last minute. What happened?" I worried.

"It's what's going to happen. Here's what I need you to do. You need to put on your coat, and get into your car and find a supermarket. You're in civilization up there, so that should be easy even at nine o'clock on a Saturday night. I want you to go inside and buy me a box of Drake's 'Ring-Dings'… a BIG box". Ring-Dings. The man wanted me to buy some kind of snack cakes?

"And don't bother coming down here unless you have a nice big box with you. I've been dying for some Ring-Dings for days. Then it hit me. You're coming back so you can bring them."

This was the emergency? For some strange reason I found myself grinning and agreeing. My husband, hearing my half of the conversation, was shaking his head in denial over what was about to occur. As I hung up the phone, I confirmed his disbelief.

"I'm going our to find a convenience store. Does anyone want to join me?"

My confused hosts declined, but made me a map to find the closest store. My husband grumbled, but put on his coat anyway and handed me the car keys. A few blocks later and I discovered his reason for giving in and even joining me. When I reached for the only box of

Ring-Dings in the store, my husband was also reaching. In his case it was for his own preferred style of snack cake from the Drake folks called, of all things, 'Yodels'.

"Hey, if you can get Andre some Ring Dings then I can get some Yodels," he responded to my raised eyebrows as the cashier rang up the purchase. "And I don't know how you think we're going to get these home but my Yodels better not get crushed."

Master packer that I was, neither man was disappointed one day and three thousand miles later. I'd felt bad the next morning as we quietly left our sleeping hosts behind at five in the morning to catch our early flight home. We'd spent so little time with them and yet they'd been so kind. And, they had barely laughed over the Ring-Dings and Yodels. I knew they'd fit right in living on St. John.

Bob and I were anxious to get back home to peace and quiet and the same bed every night. Before the plane from Boston left the ground we'd made a firm decision to take our next vacation in Arizona or New Mexico. In fact, anywhere where we knew no one and had no obligations and had no schedules to keep would be nice. We'd had enough of holidays for the moment, and we had commitments back in St. John to keep.

Bob and I had started an Adopt A Trail group. It began innocently enough when a casual conversation turned our thoughts to the VI National Park that covers two-thirds of the island. The National Park survives on a tiny budget, with little monies available for upkeep and maintenance. Since the Virgin Islands is allowed only non-voting

Delegates in Washington, trading votes with other State Representatives to get the Park budget increased is near impossible. Since Bob wanted to hike and I needed the exercise, we thought it would be a good idea to do some volunteer work at the same time. We'd seen Adopt A Trail programs in other National Parks and given the financial crunch the VI National Park Service lived with, it made sense to try. When Bob mentioned it to our neighbors, they were enthusiastic to join in. It grew from there.

We settled on the Brown Bay Trail, mostly because Andre and Bob went for a hike there one day and came back enthusiastic. In its entirety the trail is pretty rugged and long. But the portion from the East End road to the beach on Brown Bay was reasonable, they both agreed. It was overgrown but still passable and led to a rather remote beach. In just two weeks, twelve friends had decided to participate. Everyone signed the park-required volunteer forms and we were ready to begin, or so we thought. The only day that everyone seemed to have off from work on a regular basis was Sundays. This would make it difficult to get on-site assistance from Park personnel, but we were determined.

That first day we made it to the trailhead at eight o'clock in the morning. Since we all lived on the other side of the island, we got up very early to make it there in time, and it showed. A few of us brought machetes, and even fewer knew how to use them. Bob and I had received our "his" and "her" machetes for Christmas from our friend Dan in New England and we were anxious to try them out. No one had work gloves and quite a few people wore T-shirts and shorts, as they didn't own long pants. Still, Bob thought he was very prepared. On principle he carried a huge backpack loaded with towels, water, emergency first aid kits, etc. He should have brought more Band-Aids.

The first third of the trail was uphill all the way. The kids from Colorado in our group were annoying as their twenty-something bodies bounced up the trail with little effort. I was winded within the first five minutes, but at least I wasn't alone in my pain. Everything was overgrown and in some places it was hard to believe there was a path at all. Both Bob and Andre received much ribbing for their interpretation that the trail was 'passable'. A Park Ranger had joined us for a short time on that first day to teach us how to use the park-loaned tools safely and to provide advice, but even he was smart enough to take up the rear.

"Start at the top of the ridge," he encouraged us "and leave the beginning of the trail alone for a while. That will discourage tourists from going on the trail until it's in better shape. Perhaps I can get the Park to use heavy equipment to clear the first part at some point." It wasn't exactly a promise, but a pipe dream we all hung on to for a long time.

We learned to use and abuse our machetes that day and although the Ranger suggested working a small section of the trail at one time, once he left everyone hacked their way to the beach. We needed that sense of accomplishment. There were no plants that needed protection we'd been told. "Just be careful of the thorns." And there were billions of thorns that scratched us all. On the way we encountered baby goats in the bushes and even a donkey munching in a ravine. Andre detoured everyone for a few minutes to see the old plantation gravestone he'd discovered, of a little child who was the sole occupant in the elaborate but decaying graveyard.

The final stretch to the remote Brown Bay beach was littered with old piles of broken conch shells, discarded by the fishermen who occasionally worked this area. Jessie was first to discard her outer clothes on the sandy crescent of beach and to head for the water. It was shallow for a long way out and much of the shoreline was lined with a bed of sea grass, home to thousands of baby conch. The fish were bountiful, but what blew us all away was how close the island of Tortola seemed from this north-facing beach. We knew that after the abolition of slavery on Tortola in 1838, some slaves from St. John made their way across the rough currents of the Sir Francis Drake Passage that separates the islands. It was easy to envision slaves picking this very spot in Brown Bay from which to make those desperate swims to freedom.

We ate an early lunch and refreshed from our swims, hauled our gear back up the overgrown trail only to collapse in fatigue at our vehicles on the other side of the ridge. All committed to return the next week and then every other week until the trail was up to official park specifications. But two people never returned. And one of our group was unknowingly injured. One of the Colorado kids had unwittingly uncovered and hacked away at a small, unusually formed Manchineel tree near the beach. Wherever this relatively rare plant was found on the island, the Park Service marked the trees with bright red paint and placed dire warning signs since a simple touch from the tree's sap could cause extreme burns. Eating its apple-like fruit was known to even cause death. Apparently, the National Park Service had overlooked this mutant Manchineel tree.

The injured Colorado kid came back the next week with his tale from the health clinic and with a local expert on native foliage. Together the found the offending Manchineel tree and the whole group cleared the surrounding area and marked the tree's presence with a small wall of broken conch shells and driftwood. Someone found some charcoal from a fisherman's beach fire and a couple of washed up pieces of plank with which to make a warning sign. Another person found a length of red plastic tape on the beach carried by wind and water from who knows where that we used to rope off the offending plant from unwary tourists. We were proud of our efforts. A couple of visits later, anyone could traverse the Brown Bay Trail without even thorn scratches from more benign foliage.

Then Dan and Jo finally made it to St. John. I wanted everything in the apartment to be perfect for their arrival. Bob figured they were so enamored with St. John and each other, my efforts didn't matter, and he refused to chip in and help. The day before they were due, I spent the whole morning cleaning to remove any lingering trace of cobwebs or dust balls that I knew could easily grow inches wide by dinner time. Halfway through putting fresh towels in the guest bathroom, the phone rang.

"Hey Buddy," my friend Dan began in apparent high spirits.

"Where are you?" I asked. "Are you ready for Paradise?"

"I was going to ask you the same thing. Where are you? Do you know what day this is?" Dan plugged on.

"Sure. I'm getting all ready for you. I'll be waiting for you at the airport tomorrow." The guy was obviously overly excited about getting here. He called me, so of course he knew where I was.

"Well, we may not still be here tomorrow. We've been waiting for you already for two hours." Did he mean what I thought he did? "At the airport," he finally added.

"But you're due tomorrow, not today. Bob wrote it on the calendar." But the itinerary we'd posted on the refrigerator door told the real truth. And the calendar was wrong. "I'm sorry, I'm really, really sorry," was all I could think to say.

"She's on island-time," I heard him chuckle as he hung up the phone.

Dan and Jo made it from St. Thomas under their own steam. A contrite and humble hostess was there to greet them on the St. John dock, babbling about island-time and how their vacation would be uphill from this point forward. They'd come for a ten day visit and were determined nothing would prevent them from living their fantasy. They did it all. Swimming and snorkeling and exploring every day as expected. Their romantic evening walk along the grounds of a lush resort was followed the next night with an even more romantic sunset dinner high up at Chateau Bordeaux overlooking Coral Bay and the East End. For both Bob and I, most days were business as usual and we were jealous.

On the only day Bob and I both had free from work, Dan and Jo wanted to treat us to a day of fun and play. Those normal pleasures of floating at a beach didn't meet their criteria of 'something special'.

So, we turned to the local newspaper for ideas. A "*FUND-RAISING FLOTILLA*", the advertisement screamed. The Moravian Church in Coral Bay was to be the beneficiary of the effort. Their history of kindness to local boaters needing shelter and assistance during hurricanes and other disasters ensured a strong turnout. Each donation provided event participants with a sailboat ride to Norman Island in the British Virgin Islands for a day of partying and beach fun. Even Bob got excited, and the next morning he bought four tickets to the event for an outlandishly small donation.

We gathered, as directed, at the dock in Coral Bay at eight o'clock in the morning to board a sailboat. It was first-come first-serve and Dan made sure to get there early. The sailboat we ended up on carried only ten people including the captain and his mate. Dave, our captain, made us feel comfortable right away and offered to let anyone volunteer help with the rigging and the steering and learn something new about sailing. Our Norman Island destination, thought by many as the site of Robert Louis Stevenson's "Treasure Island", was a three and a half-hour sail away. The boat didn't even have to make the normal detour to Tortola to clear customs. Customs agents had volunteered to meet the flotilla in a bay on Norman Island itself to handle the formalities, and again on the dock in Coral Bay, so no time would be lost from the festivities.

There were over twenty-five boats participating in the event and although ours was first out from Coral Bay, it was by no means the first one to arrive at our destination. For the queasy, powerboats were provided to make the journey a much quicker one, and some sailboats had left directly from other places, already filled with friends and relatives of the captains. On a sandy beach on Norman Island, there were tables already heavily laden with free food. T-shirts and drinks sold for a small sum to contribute to the church funds. A huge fishing boat from Maine (!) sat in the middle of the Bay, providing a stage for live music to be enjoyed by all.

We snorkeled in fabulously clear water, the surface as smooth as glass, and saw new varieties of fish and corals in amazing colors. In the food line I was surprised by how many people greeted me by name as they tried to decide between hamburgers and chips or fungi, rice with beans and other local fare. Live entertainment from the floating stage got even Dan and Jo to lift their heads out of the water a few times to check out the action. Just an occasional cloud that cooled things off for a few minutes at a time graced the sunny day. On the return trip, Dan took the wheel and piloted the boat for a while.

That night Jo and Dan told us they'd decided to move to St. John themselves in a couple of years. They didn't expect our reactions.

"You visited Maho Bay this week, didn't you?" Bob asked, catching my eye. Puzzlement was written on their faces but they agreed.

"Hmmm," I added with a smile and wouldn't say more. Dan and Jo both proceeded to babble about the reasons they'd fallen in love with the island and why it made sense to make a drastic change in their lives, but we hardly listened. Bob and I exchanged secret looks and chalked another one up to the Ethel McCully syndrome that we were now convinced was real.

The next day we took them to the Brown Bay Trail along with our motley crew of locals. Our numbers had dwindled to the core of six to eight people that managed to bring visible results to the trail. Like many volunteer groups, we'd lost enthusiasm for the hard work after our first few visits, but we kept at it. The trail had become an escape of sorts from our daily grind. While moving rocks and cutting away the jungle, we shared weekly gossip and philosophized on every topic imaginable. It might not have been a bi-weekly vacation by any stretch of the imagination, but it was therapeutic.

Since the trail's numerous thorny ketch-an-keep plants clung to me so often, I'd become known as "Ketch-An-Keep Karin". Bob was in his glory as Ranger Bob and Andre had become Machete Man. We also had the Colorado Kids, the Rake Queen, and Lopper Lady who took all her pent up aggressions out on the stubborn trail growth. Only Jessie was without a nickname until Dan came and bestowed the perfect one.

The East End of St. John is notorious for it's large free-roaming herds of goats. Jessie, the only real kid in our crew, loved to mimic their cries. "Watch this," she told Dan and Jo as we approached our first herd in Coral Bay on the way to the trailhead. "I'll make them move."

"Baaah-baaah," she intoned, and sure enough the goats moved out of the way. Dan was not impressed and told Jessie it was probably just coincidence.

"Oh, yeah? I can make them answer me," she said indignantly. Around the next curve, five goats gave her the chance to prove it. "Baaah-

baaah-baaah".

The returning chorus of "Baaah-baaah-baaah" caused raised eyebrows from all the adults.

"Lucky . . ." Dan said, which brought smiles from most, but a mild punch in the shoulder from Jessie. I pulled into the parking area at the trailhead and was greeted by three more goats wandering past. Jo asked if the goats would bother us when we got out of the car.

"No problem," said a smug Jessie. "I'll just tell them to lay down. Baaah-Baaah. Baaah," she called out and sure enough the goats moved out of our way and then lay down in the middle of the road. Everyone was amazed, but Jessie just bounced out of the car and up the trail.

Dan called out "Pretty good, Goat Girl." That was it. The name stuck and whenever the Adopt-A-Trail group got together, it just wasn't the same unless Goat Girl made the trip.

Bob's mom and other family members arrived in St. Thomas for a one-day visit during a cruise just a couple of days after Dan and Jo left town. Rather than attempting to get to St. John for a few hours, his mom wrangled an invitation for Bob and I to join them on the ship while it was in port. It was our first experience on a large cruise ship. We got to the dock early and observed the slow process of docking and disembarking of the day-trippers. On board, we got a tour and spent the day relaxing and catching up. Bob's folks were relieved to see us so happy and healthy and the reverse was true. It was disappointing that we couldn't show them our home but before the end of the day they promised to visit St. John for a week the following year.

The visit had made an unlikely impact on Bob who'd always demurred from taking a cruise himself. He'd convinced himself he'd be bored and spend all his time eating. A visit to the health club, a walk around the running track and the pools, and a look at a typical daily activity schedule made the difference. Bob suggested we take our first cruise before the year was out, to visit other Caribbean islands and 'check out the neighborhood'. He was determined to vacation where it was warm.

One night when we were having dinner on our porch with a couple who'd lived on St. John for a few years, the conversation naturally turned to the hectic tourist season and local craziness. The tourists who seemed to have invaded Cruz Bay, making it difficult to park in town and making ferry rides always a crowded affair, added regular color to our normally dull lives. I commented that I thought it was our duty to be nice to every tourist, even if we were having a bad day.

"Then I guess I shouldn't tell you about my almost decking a tourist from the ferry," said the normally sweet and bubbly Mary seated next to me. We had to hear this one, and so encouraged Mary related her sordid tale. It all started when she was returning to St. John one afternoon after a hot frustrating morning measuring canvas awnings for a client and picking up a shipment of cushions that was a staple item for their manufacturing business. The foam cushions had arrived days late, and production was behind schedule. Ferrying the materials to St. John was the only alternative to get them into the shop without further delay. The hourly ferry was overflowing with tourists and luggage all heading for a week of fun on St. John and, as is normally the case, the ferry crew required all luggage and packages to be left dockside and be loaded onto the ferry by crewmen.

Mary was very paranoid that her shipment would get soiled and begged the crew to be extra careful, but they treated the foam as roughly as they did everything else they hauled onto the boat. Twenty minutes later, Mary attempted to take the cushions with her as she left the boat. "No!" she was yelled at. It was a nice attempt, but she should have known better than to even try. After all of the passengers disembarked, the crew formed a human chain and tossed stored items piece by piece onto a pile on the dock. Mary's customized foam cushions landed in the middle of the pile. To add insult to the situation, a big brawling tourist began to climb over the pile to retrieve his own luggage without waiting for it to be all sorted out.

"Stop it please!" shouted Mary, as she reached for his arm. The man continued his own hunt, stepping all over one of my friend's cushions.

"Those are my cushions you're stepping on," she said through clenched teeth.

"Bug off!" was the answer Mary heard, as the tourist stepped onto another of the cushions to get better leverage.

"Wanna bet?" Mary snarled as she snapped. With a right hook, she wound up to squarely punch the man in the face and knock him off the pile. Luckily for her, Mary's husband had come down to the ferry dock to help her carry her load and at that moment quickly extracted Mary and her cushions from what had become an ugly situation.

"When did this all occur?" I asked in a sweet voice.

"Six weeks ago, so I think we're safe," Mary said. The whole incident was so out of character, we all chuckled.

"Great. I hope the guy didn't get your name or the name of your business. Any day now we're going to read a letter to the Editor in *Conde Naste Traveler* or *Caribbean Life* complaining about the unfriendliness of the natives and it will probably make headline news in the local paper".

"Mary needs a vacation," Bob murmured after they left. Everybody does all the time, I thought.

Chapter Thirteen

Going with the Flow

In between visitors and holidays, our time was spent more serenely in the daily existence that makes St. John special. A romantic dinner took little effort whenever Bob or I wanted it. Plugging in the Christmas lights that lined our porch railing and adding two wind-protected candles was all it took to add ambiance to our outdoors dining room. Our sunsets were always spectacular. When the sun set, the nighttime lights of St. Thomas in the distance and a background chorus gratis of nature's nightlife made our porch a very private Paradise. Later, we often lay in our hammock in the dark and watched the stars spanning the heavens. We never experienced such spectacular shows of nature in the States. St. John nights always made us want to linger, even more than our redwood swing set in New England. And we never lost the awe our private views inspired.

It had been three months since I'd bought the funky coconut bird feeder, made by a local artisan near Salt Pond Bay, that hung from the edge of the porch. My island neighbors assured me that a little sugar water in the bottom would quickly attract lots of birds. With two cats, and a memory of the timid birds in New England, I wasn't hopeful. Even considering island-time, I was overdue in giving it a try. Within minutes of adding the sugar water mixture one morning, a lone bananaquit was perched on the edge, enjoying a morning snack.

When I glanced out in mid-afternoon, there were no less than six bananaquits crowded around the feeder with lots more chirping in the bushes nearby. I looked for my cats. The princess was enthralled. She was seated on a table just five feet away, staring with disbelief and with joy. Having no experience killing birds, she was content to sit back and just watch. Our outdoor adventurer couldn't be bothered. The birds were too small and too fast for his tastes and besides, he'd cornered a small lizard at the end of the porch. Priorities were priorities.

Bob's regular weekend priority was to find beach privacy. He liked the idea of nude sunbathing, but only with great discretion, since that activity is illegal on St. John. We discovered that adjacent to many beaches were small sandy coves that were out of view and inaccessible except by swimming or by boat. Not to be deterred, we'd pack everything in waterproof containers or dry bags, tie them to a swimming float to take a short swim to complete privacy. We didn't rough it on these occasions. We'd float a beach umbrella, snorkeling gear, books, cooler with lunch, and even binoculars and a camera.

Then Bob and I bought a kayak. The only surprise was that it took Bob so long to convince me to do it. The kayak was a used heavy plastic one, designed for two people to sit on top. Gear was meant to be hauled using ropes and the tie-downs attached at various points throughout the length of the boat. Unfortunately, the kayak had seen better days. The tie-downs were loose in some places and missing in others, leaving small holes that made it easy for water to get into the boat.

"A simple ratchet tool and some new rivets will fix it," Bob assured me.

It took months to find a ratchet tool that worked. Nowhere on St. Thomas or St. John could he find ratchets of the right size to do the job. A business trip to the States and a stateside hardware store were needed before the problem was solved and we could kayak to guarantee our beach privacy.

Finding tools and hardware was a tiny part of the local shopping challenge. You may recall hearing in the news that the landmark J.W. Woolworth's Company had closed its doors nationwide across the U.S. forever. On the mainland its passing went unnoticed by many. Everyone on St. John felt the store closing on St. Thomas. This Woolworth's had been a profitable store, frequented by most everyone. Only a K-Mart remained to provide a full variety of everyday items at reasonable prices. Rumors quickly spread of some company to fill Woolworth's space. Everyone had a favorite to fill his or her personal desires. In the end, K-Mart decided to open a second store. So much for competition.

My business trips off island had dropped to a reasonable every six weeks or so, while I'd become the neighborhood conduit for odd purchases that were difficult to obtain in the Tropics. On one trip I brought back a purple plastic ski jacket zipper for Bev's local dry cleaning company, a stainless steel clamp for Matthew, a paperback book sought after by Jay, and the inevitable Ring Dings and Yodels for Andre and Bob. Of course, I regularly brought back odd grocery items that were priced much cheaper in the States. I was not alone in this endeavor. Every time someone took a trip off-island, even if it was just to St. Thomas, offers to procure needed items were given. Always it was with the understanding that the goods would be purchased only if the time, availability, prices and transportation made sense.

As an avid reader I had anticipated books would be scarce on St. John. The island had a single small bookstore with retail prices outside the range of a ferocious reader. My paranoia was unfounded. Others shared my pleasures and a round-robin approach to book lending became the norm. Occasional additions of recent releases came courtesy of Birdie or visiting friends from off-island. Pickles Deli and the Sea Breeze Café in Coral Bay were two of the many businesses that offered a free bookshelf where passing tourists left an occasional gem. I sometimes recycled books of my own by adding to these collections.

Local ways were often painful to the uninitiated. Someone educated us with a tale about Mark and Marsha, St. John residents for a few years, and the house they were building on the island. While many tried to convince them that the difficulties and delays they'd experience weren't worth it, Mark was determined to succeed. His roof was halfway completed when the roofer didn't show up for work one day. When found at a local bar, the roofer said the weather called for showers so he couldn't work, but he'd be back the next day. That next day was a perfect one weather-wise. There was a nice breeze all day. Occasional high clouds brought regular relief from the normally hot island sun. Yet, the roofer again didn't show up. Neither did the plumber, who'd been dependable up to now.

Three days later the roofer returned to the site and continued work as though there'd been no delay. The owner was furious, and demanded reasons for the delay. Wary of the owner's anger, the roofer mumbled his explanation. The weather had gotten so good that he'd gone sailing down-island for a couple of days.

"First the roofer, then the plumber," Mark growled mostly to himself, "at least one of them is back." The roofer, overhearing, grinned.

"No problem. The plumber, he be here soon," the roofer assured the owners. "We'd be on his boat."

Believe it or not, the roofer and the plumber helping to build the house had 'good' reputations as being dependable. Their behavior was acceptable within the local culture and their job skills beyond reproach. Our friend learned the hard way that adapting to island ways could be detrimental to the sanity of any relocated continental.

Bob and I had initially shied away from buying food at the numerous small food booths located around town, primarily because no one ever posted signs to explain what was for sale. Sheila, who lived in a little house near our apartment, ran a small booth called Sheila's Pot directly across the street from the ferry docks in Cruz Bay Park and she always seemed busy. When I finally got past concerns that my queries would be considered rude, I asked her why she didn't put up signs.

"Wouldn't you sell more if you did?" I asked naively.

"If it's good, you don't need to," she scolded me with a smile as she offered me some chicken soup for my little cold. "Every day, I sell out," she explained. I was going to suggest that she could make and sell even more if she put up signs, but I already knew what she'd say. Sheila cooked what she could make, transport via a taxi and store under her small downtown stall. Any more would have meant increasing her overhead for a car, more storage and more help. Then she wouldn't be able to 'lime away' the time with her customers and it just wouldn't be Sheila's Pot any more.

Whenever I had to send a fax, I'd pass by Sheila's Pot and say "Good Morning". My company headquarters opened late in the morning by St. John standards, so morning was a good time to run errands in town. The seasonal only daylight savings time change in the states meant it was mid-morning before I could reach anyone by phone. St. John never adjusted its clocks, as most didn't feel the need to add this kind of stress to their lives. For me, it meant early morning hours were relaxed, but it added a challenge when working with folks on the West Coast by phone, and I longed for everyone else to 'spring back' to normal.

Most work was done via computer. To log into my computer at my company's headquarters, I connected my notebook computer to our apartments telephone line, dialed the long distance number and with luck, got through without a Spanish recording telling me the circuits were busy. Then I used a credit card sized device my company had given me to get past the computer security and log in and begin my workday.

The little security device died one day. It meant that I could not get my e-mail for at least a week, as I couldn't get through my company's security checkpoints. The company said they had to verify my problem before they would send a replacement by mail. They would make no exceptions to by-pass their security processes. It took over two days arguing just to get them to agree the device had indeed stopped working and I needed a new one sent by Post Office Express Mail, which took three days to arrive on-island. I had to do most work via telephone or fax in the interim. I could only imagine the disruption a hurricane would cause on my work-life. Then telephones and faxes might not be an option.

Anxious to catch up on my e-mails, I'd locked both cats outdoors for once, closing the screen door behind them. I needed uninterrupted work time without risk of a cat jumping onto the keyboard for attention and soon I was involved, not noticing the time fly by until my shoulders began to ache. As I broke my focus from the screen in front of me, something swooped by through the air. The instant thought that came as I cringed in fear was that a piece of the overhead fan had broken loose. But, there was no crashing sound. I looked up and noticed nothing wrong at first. Then I saw 'it' up in the master bedroom loft, precariously circling the large ceiling fan and swooping down towards the bed occasionally to find a way out.

I ran up the stairs opening the living room screen door on my way. Both cats had to jump back for safety before they quickly bounced inside. They had pasted themselves on the screen to watch the tantalizing show I'd been too oblivious to notice. For perhaps two hours I'd had a hummingbird in my house. Opening the screen door in the bedroom had no effect, nor did turning off the fan. The bird only flew in larger circles, until it was swooping down to circle the large living room fans.

My cats thought it was all great fun. They'd both sat down on the middle of the living room couch and were watching with awe. I opened the remaining doors in the apartment, turned off the downstairs fans, and watched helplessly as the bird continued his efforts. Now he explored everywhere, confused by where the wind had gone. It was one of those rare days when there were no trade winds blowing on-island. Without the fans, it was hot. Both cats were panting with their tongues hanging out, but probably for different reasons than the heat. It was a long half-hour before I'd coaxed the hummingbird out of the house. The cats proceeded to play dead on the living room floor, in disappointment or from heat exhaustion, and wouldn't move until I turned on their ceiling fans again.

After a good rain, the hummingbirds would take baths in the water filled leaves of an almond tree that climbed beside the porch. Unlike the early winter months, there was a lot of rain in early spring. Every week some different flower came into bloom and a new exotic perfume filled the air. My garden on the porch finally began to take shape. A rooting from an asparagus fern, bromliads, a couple of small palm trees, a ficus, some hanging ivy and a wandering jew started from cuttings, anthuriums gratis of my landlord, and a lone orchid received as a gift - all gave our porch a decidedly cozy feel. My husband began training the ever-present bougainvillea nearby to weave gracefully through the porch railing. We were growing a natural sun barrier that would minimize the hot afternoon heat all summer.

My landlord gave me a couple of tomato seedlings, and visions of a heavy crop of fresh fruit filled my brain. The tomato plants grew unbelievably fast. When they bloomed with yellow blossoms covering the tops of each plant my excitement mounted. While watering them, I would think back on our lives in New England and how visits in the summer months with neighbors often included an offer of strawberries or squash, or tomatoes. Especially the tomatoes.

But, my own efforts at growing began to prove that 'stick the seedling in the ground and stand back' wasn't an approach that would work in Paradise. I'd encountered new species of insects and fungus that threatened my plants and 'blossom drop' which no local suggestions seemed to solve. Bob was supportive, even testing the idea that the plants needed cooler nighttime weather by bringing the heavy pots into the apartment and placing them in an air-conditioned room for a few nights. Nothing worked. For months I hung on to my bug infested but constantly flowering plants before finally giving in to the inevitable.

Whenever I got really depressed over hoping for my own vine ripened tomato, someone else's bounty soon made me forget the desire. A finger of fat short little bananas, a pile of guavas, mangos, limes, and even herbs would arrive gratis from some local friend. They were as grateful that we took these gifts, as we were appreciative of receiving them. When a banana tree bears fruit, it bears a lot. I experimented with local fruits, including them occasionally in recipes I'd previously restricted to New England grown bounty. Besides, bananas and mangos were good picnic fare for the beach but we always seemed to have too much. So we shared whenever we could find a willing tourist.

Like most people on St. John, we truly appreciated the tourists who made downtown parking difficult and crowded our restaurants and beaches. They kept the island fresh and alive and made us smile. Bob and I liked to make the tourists grin and they did regularly when we offered to take their pictures with their cameras. At the beach, it the park in restaurants, on the dock - we met fascinating people that way. On the white sandy beaches, I loved to share island trivia.

"Do you know what makes all this beautiful white sand?" I would ask. Often the answer was "No", but some offered "the waves breaking the coral" or "broken sea shells" or "rocks being worn ways." All these things were true, but much of our beaches came from a very different source.

"Parrot Fish Poop," I would respond with a laugh. The looks on people's faces were amazing as I suggested they float face down in the water when snorkeling and watch it happen. Often, they'd follow my suggestion and then stop back by with grins and agreement at their new discovery.

The local pig roasts and beach parties that were often held on palm-tree lined Oppenheimer Beach on the north shore were the activities that got Bob and I playing like tourists. The small house right on the beach owned by the Territorial government was a popular site for events since the building - with its broad porch, steps leading directly into the water, a kitchen and two bathrooms - could be rented for a nominal fee to private parties. Special events meant cars lined the narrow National Park road above the property, but at the most upscale parties, gratis open air transportation was provided from Hawksnest Beach where parking is more abundant. A truckload of borrowed Tiki lamps provided lighting for evening extravaganzas. Sometimes the events were very private like a wedding or birthday party and some were fund-raisers for some good cause. Often they were word of mouth parties where a bunch of locals got together and rented the space just for an excuse to enjoy a day at the beach.

Life was not always fun and parties or even too mundane on St. John. There was the occasional crisis, whether imagined or real, to shake up our world. One quiet day, my neighbor Sheila was at my door, calling out "Inside – Inside". It took me a minute to remember that some folks on St. John still lived in places that had no doors and that calling 'Inside' was a culturally proper alternative to knocking.

"Inside – Kah-rrin', are you d'ere?" Sheila called again in an urgent way. Her propane tank had just been filled, and now the smell of leaking propane was overpowering in her small home up the hill from our apartment. She was afraid of an explosion. I quickly lent her the phone, but it wasn't much help, as I had no idea what to do. Luckily a friend of Sheila's drove by my open door at that minute and offered to check out the problem. He found that the tank had been filled so completely, the sun pouring down on the exposed tank had expanded the gas and it had no where to go but out the safety valve built-in for this purpose.

A building running out of cistern water was a more common trau-matic event for everyone on St. John, since it meant no water for flushing toilets, taking showers or cleaning dishes until the water trucks came. It was the tropical version of the wintertime disaster in New England of running out of oil for the furnace. And it cost a small fortune for a water delivery truck that could provide just enough water for a month or so of no rain. Unless someone sinned, as they did in Andre's apartment building one day.

The building had just gotten a water delivery a week earlier but sud-denly the cistern was empty again. Everyone assumed a leak in the cistern below the house caused the problem. Moe, our landlord, didn't find this theory amusing or likely. He personally checked out the building inside and out to get answers and growled at everyone. It turned out that a new tenant had a toilet that sometimes didn't stop flushing completely. Without realizing the problem this could cause, the tenant had left town for ten days with his toilet continuously leaking water. Eight thousand gallons of water had escaped in one short week without anyone noticing.

Unfortunately our water bills weren't tax deductible. It was tax sea-son. Bob and I found a local accountant, Maureen, to help us survive income tax season. She also played a base cello in a band we often listened to on Friday nights at the Tamarind Inn. With her guidance we learned about the nuances in the tax codes which made it advan-tageous for us to live and work in the USVI. We also paid a bundle for our sins in the past year. Even so, when it was all over, Bob and I had a little money left over to step up our efforts to play in Paradise and so we did.

With two other couples, we rented a powerboat for the day. We tooled around St. John with each of the men taking a turn at piloting. Only one of us had any real experience with powerboats, but luckily, the seas were extremely calm that day, and everyone's confidence was high. We pulled very close to the point at Ram's Head to make a quick snorkeling stop. Normally, the waves crash harshly against the high cliffs there on the south shore, so it was a rare opportunity to explore. I felt very under control when Andre said the depth gage told us there was still fourteen feet of water, although we were very close to the rocky shore. Later I discovered there was no depth gauge on the boat. It was merely the RPM reading Andre had been quoting. Despite the fact that we were well off shore and the sun was high in the sky by then, my whole body shuddered.

We went to Norman Island in the British Virgin Islands for lunch. Our restaurant was a floating ship anchored in a quiet harbor. It was a crowded place. The drinks were strong and the food hearty. Halfway through our cheeseburgers, Bob's boss and his wife popped on board from a small inflatable skiff with an outboard motor. They'd come over from St. John just for lunch. It is very unusual for anyone to cross even that small stretch of sea in such a tiny craft, but with the rare calm waters it was easy to envision someone water-skiing all the way to St. Croix that day.

Over time, Bob and I became savvy on the local boating regulations. As knowledgeable locals, we got steamed when pleasure seekers were too inept or determined to break the rules, especially when they anchored boats too close to shore or blocking the marked entry channels. Often it was effective to simply comment out loud, "I hope the Coast Guard doesn't catch those boat people outside the markers. They'll get into a lot of trouble. Did you know that they might even get their boats confiscated?" Moments later if luck was with us, the boats would move on to other, less public waters. Unfortunately this strategy didn't always work and I cringed whenever I realized these stupid people were destroying the reefs and shoreline that had brought them to this place.

Maybe the policeman, too, cringed when I parked illegally across from the Post Office one day. Parking in town was always a challenge, but I was blissfully unaware I was breaking the law. My Geo Tracker found a rare open parking space in the lot along the road facing the Post Office on its first loop through the lot. The ferry was about to leave for St. Thomas and I considered myself lucky. Upon returning three hours later, my first parking ticket was waving on the windshield.

"Parking in a thirty minute parking zone," read the indictment. But I'd parked in this same lot a hundred times without getting a ticket before. It took me long minutes of searching to find the 'posted sign' that had been remarked about on the ticket. Even so, it took a scrubbing from a rag in my car to wipe the grime off the sign and decipher its warning. Apparently this one row of parking slots was earmarked for short term parking while the rest of the lot was up for grabs. And yet, the car next to mine had been parked there before mine, but had no ticket. I felt like an outsider.

Two wrongs don't make a right, I reminded myself. I was in the wrong and decided to pay the ticket right away. It was a new adventure in island ways. The policeman had written on the ticket to pay at the Boulon Center. So, I went there only to be confronted with a locked door and a sign informing all that this was indeed the place to pay fines of various sorts, but that the next time it would be open for business was three weeks away. I would be out of town on business by the time the office opened again, so I took a short walk to our fine new police headquarters a block away.

It was my first time in this new building which had been officially open for only a short while. I was impressed by the thick bulletproof glass partition and encouraged by the smiling officer behind the barrier. Walking right up to the grill placed at an awkward height, I offered to pay my fine directly to him, since the Boulon Center office was closed. He told me the ticketing officer was wrong and probably from St. Thomas, whatever that meant. Nervously, as he eyed the new overhead security camera, he said they didn't take monies at the station and redirected me to the Motor Vehicle Inspection Lane down the road. At the Motor Vehicle place, I was assured parking tickets could be paid. However, the computers were down and it was suggested that I return the next day.

That next day, I made sure I had cash along with a blank check, and even a credit card to cover all possibilities. One of the girls behind the desk told me there was a little problem. The girl who is allowed to take monies was out on break and wouldn't be back for an hour or more. Despondent, I headed home only to pass Jay's place of work where she too was taking a break and motioned for me to stop and chat for a moment. When I told her about my parking ticket, she just rolled her eyes and laughed. Most people didn't bother to pay tickets right away. They just waited until their yearly inspection was due. Then, the computer would show they had outstanding fines and everyone either paid up in full or sold the car to some unsuspecting person who would have to pay them before the car could be registered. Jay bet me five dollars that I wouldn't be able to pay it on my next try.

Two hours later I was back at her workplace to pay off my lost bet and kill a little more time. At the Motor Vehicle place, the girl who took the cash was back in the office, but she wouldn't take my money, because the girl who was responsible for writing out the receipt was at lunch. My luck changed an hour later after returning from my aimless wander around town. It took two minutes from beginning to end to actually pay my parking ticket and get a receipt. That's when I learned about the confusing signs posted on the road that ran between the cemetery and the beach across the street in Cruz Bay. There was a sign facing town that read "No parking from 8:00 AM to 6:00 PM Mon-Fri" while on the other side of the same sign-pole was another directive. This one read "No Parking" and nothing more.

All the way home I fantasized about every law breaker getting ticketed and paying their fines right away and how the local government would then have a surplus of funds available to improve efficiencies and signage and make the world a better place. But closing my car door, my last thought was "never happen", and my mind moved off to thoughts of a quiet evening in Paradise.

Bob and I had just settled into our bed for the night. Flashing lights reflecting off our bathroom window roused us from our sleep along with the unusual sounds of gathered people. My husband went to the window guessing it was probably the police ticketing the car that had sat at the side of the road for weeks. "It's a fire!" he called out. Rushing to his side, I saw fire trucks and firemen milling about as they attempted to extinguish a transformer fire at the top of the electrical pole near our building. No matter what they did, they could barely reach the source of the fire high up on the pole. Our electricity went off as the firefighters sought to gain control. There was a strong wind that night and we immediately thought about the possibility the fire might spread.

After a few minutes the firemen seemed to have the situation under control. Without the constantly moving bedroom fan, the room was stifling so I went onto the balcony where I could no longer see the firemen at work. Over my shoulder I could barely see the pink fire glow in the black night. I saw a red spark falling to the dry ground below and assumed my neighbors were also awake and someone had thrown a cigarette butt off their balcony. It annoyed me that they would be so inconsiderate since the ground was so dry from lack of rain. But then, looking in the distance I saw two, then five, then even more red glows, floating downwards some hundreds of yards down the gut, or ravine, below our property. My neighbors weren't smoking. The wind was sending sparks across the gut and I realized the situation was still a dangerous one. A restless hour later, the fire was out and luckily no other fires appeared below our house.

The next morning I discussed the previous night's excitement with my Parrot-Head neighbor, surrounded by Jimmy Buffet memorabilia, who lived in a studio apartment diagonally below mine. It was a wild event, she agreed, then assured me that the firemen were as conscientious as possible with the sparks the night before.

With a shrug, Pam told me she awoke from the commotion, but stayed inside until the fire was almost out. Unfortunately in the dark night, my friend had lit a cigarette before she climbed the short stairway to the street to check out the aftermath. A firefighter, seeing only the red glow on the side of the stairway, drenched Pam with his hose. Our stout concrete walls prevented Bob and I from seeing or hearing this calamity. My Parrot-Head friend wasn't angry at all with the firemen.

"They were just doing their job," she admitted with a wry grin.

"At least they brought their own water," I added. I'd begun to think like a St. Johnian, accepting the bizarre without a thought, but with thoughts of precious water always in my consciousness.

"And the lawn and bushes got a nice free soaking," my friend finished for me with a smile and a flick as she lit up another cigarette.

Not everyone on St. John had the amenities that those living in our building did. Some even lived without electricity or even four walls to call home. Exploring the East End of the island in our kayak one day, Bob and I encountered numerous remote sandy coves, accessible only by small watercraft and hidden from the eyes of larger boats. With occasional paddling we drifted from one to another, each more picturesque than the last. Rounding a small outcrop of rocks, we discovered one tiny cove that was spectacular. Bob murmured that this would be the ideal place to hang it up and live off the land. The cove was edged in a shallow reef on one side and sea grass on the other, while the center was pure white sand leading up to a perfect beach. Sea grapes and Palm trees lined the beach and rising from the steep hills on one side I could see a mighty Papaya tree. But then there was more.

Bob noticed that tucked almost out of sight there was evidence that someone, at least until recently, had been living a remote life in the bush with the most minimal of goods. A hammock, boards for a bench, an old wooden cable spool for a table and a well-used grill were our first hints. A pile of recently crushed conch shells, the remains of a fire, and coconut and mango remains nearby the beautiful but tiny remote beach told more of the story.

It can be done, I thought, as we let the lazy current take us away with the flow and on to another undiscovered patch of Paradise for our own respite that day.

St. John Trivia from 1955

From <u>The West Indies and Caribbean Year Book</u> 1956-57, Publisher -Thomas Skinner & Co. LTD, London:

- *"Education is compulsory for every child between the ages of 6 and 15 unless he or she has completed the sixth grade sooner."*
- *"Two little settlements, Cruz Bay and Coral Bay, mark the eastern and western ends of St. John and account for about 200 of its population." [population 747]*
- *"On high Bordeaux Mountain there still remains a bay tree forest where many leaves are picked for bay rum. St. John is still the main source of supply of bay leaves for the manufacture of St. Thomas Bay Rum."*
- *"The island of St. John has been declared by the Rockefeller Foundation to be one of the two places in the world free from the common cold."*

Chapter Fourteen
Peculiarities in Paradise

I'd heard about the phosphorescence in the waters long before ever experiencing the phenomena. Probably I'd been seeing this strange occurrence without even knowing it, when an evening ferry home to St. John coincided with the new moon. On those nights, when the lack of moon glow made the night especially dark, I'd noticed that if the seas were choppy, whitecaps could be seen a good distance away from the ferryboat. But, not until I'd experienced the phosphorescence at Cinnamon Bay, did I pay closer attention and notice that the whitecaps actually glowed in the dark during these nights.

Cinnamon Bay, one of the larger bays on the north shore of St. John, is the site for the island's largest campground. Bob and I had camped here for ten days on a vacation to Paradise many years ago. Since our move, we'd almost ignored this wonderful place, except to attend special events held on the premises. When the seas were up, the waves could be rough and we preferred our bathing sites to be as calm as a pond.

St. John Rescue was asked to provide on-site assistance for an 'enhancement weekend' at Cinnamon Bay Campground geared towards at-risk kids and their single parent households from St. Thomas. Most participants would be camping out for the first time, and Bob and I were asked to stay overnight in the campground along with the families. It turned out to be a very memorable experience.

The parents and children were appreciative of the smallest gesture of kindness. A peaceful day passed with the only injury being a scraped toe in need of a Band-Aid. Bob offered alcohol swabs to a diabetic minister who'd forgotten his own supply and I soothed a crying child who'd forgotten where her mom was. But, for the most part we weren't needed. As the sun set, we interacted more freely with the campers. Most participants had no idea how to start up the propane fed lanterns that marked the entrance to each tent site and a mother asked for assistance. Enlisting a young 'lieutenant' from the motley crew of children nearby, my assistant and I quickly solved her problem.

Seconds later, we were asked to do the same for another lantern on the other side of the group camping area. Before that lantern could be lit, we were inundated with additional requests. My 'lieutenant' was a big help, as he introduced me to the campers and led me through the various tent sites. Before it was over, I'd lit over twenty lanterns and was a minor heroine.

Bob, meanwhile, remained at our own site, and began getting requests for cups of ice. Every child needed at least a cup of ice to take to their bed that evening, initially to suck as a treat, and later for the inevitable drink of water they'd want late into the night. Returning from my own chore, Bob was surrounded by six toddlers holding out their cups and looking overwhelmed. I began to help him, while chatting with the children. With each handout, I reminded the children to say thank you, which brought wide eyes from some, but smiles and "t'ank yo" to Bob from all. Thank goodness the ice chest the VI National Park Service had provided us was large. We must have given out fifty cups of ice before the campground quieted for the night.

The evening was too young for Bob and I to consider turning in for the night. We took a walk down to the beach where two chairs had been left out overlooking a rocky barrier to the shoreline. It was dark and peaceful as we sat watching the sky filled with more stars than we had ever noticed before. Occasionally a meteor flashed by, adding momentary excitement. But it was the water that captured my attention within a few minutes. There was no surf that night, yet out of the corner of my eyes, I caught a movement of some sort. I began searching the waters and was rewarded with a sudden glow like a green light bulb being turned on and then off from underneath the waters surface. A few minutes later it happened again in two different spots in the water. The glow was obviously caused by nocturnal fish of some kind.

Neither Bob nor I felt sleepy. We lived almost five minutes away from a beach, which on St. John meant a long way away. But here we were, sitting on a quiet beach in the middle of the night. So we decided to take advantage of our night away to find a quiet spot for a midnight dip. We went back to the campground for Bob to get our flashlights. Then we headed out for an isolated spot on the sandy beach where we both contemplated the possibility of some illegal skinny-dipping.

My husband was barely a shadow walking away and into the calm water. Seconds later, his feet were surrounded momentarily by an eerie glow. The glow dissipated as soon as it started, as my eyes caught Bob's stilled silhouette. While taking my first steps into the water to follow him, I looked down. As I moved, my body churned the water and with each movement, the water glowed with thousands of tiny green lights as minute marine life attempted to escape from my path.

Bob and I sat quietly on the sandy bottom in knee-high water and pondered this new wonder. He slowly moved one hand along the surface, resulting in a wave of glowing phosphorescence. I mimicked his movement and we both sucked in our breaths. It was amazing. Each movement brought the sudden glow that was reminiscent of something seen only in a science fiction movie. We played with our microscopic friends that night for a long time, experimenting with and awed by the beauty of nature while the meteor shower overhead provided added entertainment. After that, whenever I traveled by water at night, I had new respect and admiration of the nightlife surrounding me.

Respect for our island's environment is something no one on St. John ever took lightly. While Bob and I were in the final planning stages of our move to Paradise, a major change almost occurred on the island with total disregard for the sensibilities and desires of most that lived here. This is the tale we were later told of the events:

A USVI territorial government agency, without a clear understanding of tiny St. Johnian idiosyncrasies, had decided to put a traffic light in Cruz Bay. To a vacationing visitor, it seemed like a reasonable answer to the traffic jams that occurred regularly on this island of few stop signs, a small police force, and no traffic lights. The traffic light arrived on-island the day before it was scheduled to be installed and it's arrival was all it took to start the storm.

St. Johnians were appalled. No public notice had been given, and the locals were united in their belief that a traffic light would be an eyesore that would only exasperate the traffic jam problem. Besides, the lack of traffic lights on St. John was very desirable for tourists who came here to get away from urban sights. Luckily, the Governor himself was on-island that same afternoon, for a speaking engagement. A grassroots group of outraged citizens confronted the Governor and insisted that he order the traffic light to remain uninstalled. It was amazing how fast the local grapevine worked. The Governor was overwhelmed with visible public outrage. Meanwhile his office was being inundated with faxes and phone calls insisting he act immediately. Luckily for St. John, the Governor responded and called for an immediate halt to the plans.

What came next is surely a St. John oddity. Apparently, the traffic light had been paid for and the box opened, so the equipment couldn't be returned. The three-tiered light fixture found a temporary home in some office at the Public works department, until someone came up with a better plan. The traffic light was mounted as the sole ornament high in the middle of the concrete side of a public works building. It's location, set back from the road off Gift Hill Road near the Centerline Road intersection, ensured maximum visibility to any St. Johnian who knew the story and needed reassurance that respect for our island mattered. Whether or not it was installed there as a working traffic light is a matter or debate.

Sometimes it took a combination of man and nature on St. John to create a legend. On the North Shore Road, in the VI National Park, a huge boulder has stood solitary along the shoreline side of the road for a millennium. This two-story high boulder that came to St. John via a volcanic blast that shaped our neighborhood is known as Easter Rock. The rock is a well-known landmark on the island, with a tall tale giving it its name. According to local legend, in the pre-dawn hours every Easter morning the egg-shaped rock would roll down the steep gut below and into the sea. Then it would magically roll back up into its regular spot, wet and dripping until the rising sun quickly dried it before most mortals noticed. Just before our first Easter on-island, some friends tried to convince Bob and I to join them in skipping our normal sleep and dowsing the rock at four AM so early rising tourists would not be disappointed. It was one thing to put out Easter eggs for neighborhood tots in Massachusetts for our annual Easter egg hunt, but this time we left continuing a legend to others.

While Easter Rock is an anomaly regularly pointed out to tourists, locals more often memorize the ever-present potholes on our island roads. Most of these potholes had been there for years and although our vigilant road crews often temporarily filled them in with stones and dirt, their results only lasted until an evening shower came. Then their work was washed away and sometimes replaced by small rocks fallen down from the hillsides above. Braking for potholes or fallen rocks was a clear indication to everyone that the driver was a tourist. Residents instinctively swerved to avoid any obstacle without any change in speed. Except when the bizarre occurred.

One night, a strong rainstorm and some recent construction work had toppled a huge boulder onto a seaside road. The boulder was at least ten feet high and wide enough to cover almost half of the narrow road and no small rocks or gravel gave it company. All the locals swerved around the strange sight during their normal roller coaster ride to and from town. The boulder appeared destined to become another St. John landmark. But a week later, I actually braked to a stop as I came upon the rock. The back end of a jeep was jutting out of the boulder, looking more like a monument than a car crash. On my way out of town later that day, the boulder was gone but the jeep was still there.

One day, as my car did a little dance around an abnormally large pothole, I had to jerk my car to a quick stop to avoid hitting a mamma hen and her brood of baby chicks that decided at that moment to leave their pothole nest to cross the road. In Paradise, everyone took care to never harm God's creatures, no matter how disruptive they were to our lives. I discovered just how far some people took this responsibility one night on St. Thomas.

A friend had offered to give me a ride to the Red Hook dock where I could catch the ferry home, as we were a long way away in a relatively rural area. But first, she had to remove a large ice cooler from the passenger's seat. I expected her to just transfer the container to the back of the truck, but first, she moved away from the vehicle and opened the cooler to let hundreds of little frogs escape.

"Normally I do this right away when I get here, but I was rushed tonight," she explained.

"Frogs?" was all I could think of in reply.

"Yes, it's part of our FRP... Frog Relocation Project," she chuckled. "My apartment building is designed with a nice little open air court-yard in the middle that has a small water fountain. The frogs just love that place."

"Sounds nice," was all I could think of to say.

"But have you ever heard the sounds these little guys can make? It gets so loud none of us can sleep at night. So every other night or so one of us takes a pool net and fills an ice cooler with frogs, then we relocate them out here where there's a little more space for them and peace and quiet for us."

With the empty ice cooler now in the back of the truck, my friend got into the driver's seat and then pulled a screwdriver out of her glove compartment. "This is my key," she said with a grin, as she proceeded to jimmy the screwdriver into the steering column shaft until the engine sputtered to life with a cough. In moments we were at Red Hook, where I was informed I would have to open my vehicle's door from the outside to get out of the truck. Her truck was a typical 'island car' that was falling apart inside and out but it had great brakes. Someone leaving the island had bequeathed it to her for free, and that made the clunker beautiful to both of us.

Arriving early at Red Hook meant time to stop at Senor Pizza - my favorite pizza parlor. It was housed in what had been a steel cargo container in an earlier life. A covered porch for the picnic-tabled seating area along with some green, red and white paint and the inevitable Christmas lights for ambiance disguised its origins. The pizza was great, but the place was more famously known as the home base for the VI Olympic Bobsled team. Their street-side sign displayed a picture of a bobsled while photographs on the inside walls proclaimed the workers' fame and proved the legend true.

Down the block, Duffy's Love Shack brought tourists and locals together like no other place could. The solitary bamboo structure situated in a strip mall parking lot housed plastic palm trees, and other tackiness that only seemed perfect at Duffy's. The owner was the son of the Duffy who is an intregal part of the Mamas and the Papas rock band legend. The establishment was an endless beach party. The food was always great and the drinks were wonderful. A tacky island momento came with every drink and for a little extra money each drink came in a specially designed plastic souvenir mug. For even more money, the plastic souvenir became a ceramic ones. Their souvenir T-shirt is a popular keepsake I've seen in airports throughout the US. Some St. Johnians have entire collections of coconut, monkey and parrot mugs courtesy of island guests who had a memorable evening at the Love Shack.

Skinny Legs was the gathering spot for many Coral Bay events. Beyond the bar, a bare area led to Coral Bay itself and provided a natural space for small concerts and fundraising activities. Some people insisted that this was the spot where Jimmy Buffet actually came up with the initial idea for a 'Cheeseburger In Paradise' and many insisted the burgers here were the best anywhere in the world. But, I liked the place for it's unique artwork – a hanging mobile made of driftwood titled "Lost Soles of Coral Bay". From each dangling string was a long lost sandal or shoe bottom someone had left behind.

There were other long lost souls on St. John, like those who'd created the petroglyphs tourists trekked to see on the Reef Bay Trail. Some soul-less people were rumored to have developed a marijuana plantation out in the bush on the northeast end of the island, complete with an automated irrigation system, but I never heard any rumors that they'd been caught. The local music scene was filled with soul of all kinds from the steel pan bands to the strong reggae beat that made local St. John bands a regional legend. And our churches sometimes drew in tourists attracted to the uplifting sounds of the congregation in perfect harmony.

Our roads were few and in a few relatively flat stretches some drivers had a tendency to speed. For safety's sake St. John roads included a few speed bumps. It helped to know who lived nearby or what school used to be in the area to understand why these barriers were placed in the spots where they were located. When increased traffic necessitated larger speed bumps near Cruz Bay, someone decided they weren't really bumps at all any more. The large yellow caution signs that went up proclaimed "Speed Hump" for these monstrosities. According to the underside of Bob's car, the signs were appropriate.

Island peculiarities were so plentiful on all our islands that I couldn't understand why some tour operators bordered on the mundane. On St. Thomas, a common complaint of tourists was that the tour guide told them little beyond what they'd read in their tourist guides, and stopped only where T-shirt vendors were ensconced. On St. John, some tour operators simply embellished the mundane and stopped wherever there was a rare flat stretch of road.

Often these open-air taxis with their bench seats crowded with tourists would wind their way out of town and past the switchback toward our south-shore apartment. As they passed around that last curve I would hear a variation of the inevitable "And on your left are wealthy condos each with their own private pools". Then they would slow to a stop on the level patch of road directly in front of my door, as the loudspeaker continued "and on your right is Rendezvous Bay with its million dollar villas". The drivers were always undaunted that most tourists had turned towards the left to look at my front door, hoping for a peek at a wealthy condo owner.

It was annoying. After three such tour visits in one morning, I understood how my friend Mary felt when the tourist had walked all over her cushions at the ferry dock. I was mad. That afternoon, I saw a taxi driver waiting for a fare at the Cinnamon Bay Campground. I asked him if he took tours of people past the overlook to Rendezvous Bay. His smiling nod was all I had to see. I told him he was wrong and crazy to think any of us in those apartments were rich. Yes, we were paying a premium to live there, but it took most of our money to be able to.

"Half of the apartments are studios, for goodness sake, and don't even have real refrigerators or stoves. And have you ever seen the pools?" I insisted. "They're the size of a postage stamp". I fumed.

I bit back my tongue in admitting we called them the dipping pools, for fear of adding to his tour dialogue. "Why don't you talk about the trees or the animals or something?" I asked. "You're good - a good tour guide, right?" I said, changing to another tack, "I'm sure there's something else you can think of than making up tales about how rich we all are. Tell them how all those small rusting cement mixers in front of everyone's homes is the St. Johnian's version of a lawn ornament. Maybe you can make up a story about how rusting abandoned vehicles add precious minerals into our hillsides. No one ever talks about those things."

The poor man didn't know what to say. He was amused and shocked at the same time. Now sane, I tried to save face, gave him a big smile, and said "Think about it. And keep bringing those tourists around," as I inched my way back to my car.

On my way home I decided perhaps the taxi drivers needed some help. For weeks I pondered what to do. On a business trip to the west coast of California, I found a large official looking yellow painted metal caution sign like those used on roadways to slow down traffic. On it was the words 'Iguana Crossing' with a picture of one of the critters to eliminate any confusion. Perfect, I thought. We had iguanas nearby, and although the local dogs would occasionally find iguana eggs, there were a couple of adult iguanas that the dogs had learned to leave alone. Four thousand miles that sign traveled in less than one day, yet it took months of island-time before it was hoisted in place outside our front yard.

Soon, the tourists noticed and began pointing and taking pictures whenever the taxis slowed, but no taxi driver ever included it in his tour. I should have posted the sign that I really wanted to, but which I didn't have the courage to put up: 'The Sum of the Gross Incomes of the Tenants Here Is Less Than the Salary of Your Taxi Driver'. The tourists might not have gotten the point, but it would have entertained the neighbors.

Getting a local driver's license gave me the jitters. I knew I was long overdue to apply, but the thought of the required written test made me paranoid. The test questions and answers required thinking like a local. Many continentals failed on their first attempt. I was advised by many to remember that speed limits that might appear were those posted ten years earlier, and I would need to memorize the formal names of highways on St. Croix. I was prepared to quote that one could obstruct traffic by stopping in the middle of the road to speak to a friend for only 'a little while', and that a necktie is an important safety device to be kept in the glove compartment in my open air vehicle. And I knew now that drinking while driving was not illegal, but that you could get arrested for not offering to take an injured person to their home or wherever else they wanted.

The afternoon before I took the test, three visitors and I went swimming at Trunk Bay. When we left the parking area, my small black purse with my stateside drivers' license was accidentally left on the soft-top of my Tracker. Unaware, we headed home, a good thirty-minute drive away. A couple of hours later I discovered my loss and

I panicked. I drove in the dark back to Trunk Bay with a flashlight and a prayer. The purse was nowhere to be found. Slowly I headed home with a wrenching in my gut, as my mind pictured the disaster I faced when I took my drivers' test the next morning. Without a valid license I would have to also take a driving test which, despite my perfect driving record, I knew I'd fail for some obscure reason.

About a mile from Trunk Bay, I saw a magnificent sight. My black purse was hanging from a tree over the road where some kind soul had found it and placed it in the island custom for me to find. My money, my credit card and most importantly my drivers' license were intact. I wasn't surprised. On my way back to town I saw a lone man with long dreadlocks walking along the road. I slowed to offer him a ride, but he waved me on with a smile and I could only guess he might have been my savior that night.

Bob and I came to accept dreadlocks like we came to accept that some island women were afraid to let raindrops touch their bodies. Good dreadlocks required a lot of attention and care, we discovered. And the long-standing superstition that rain on a belly would cause a child to be born sickly was something not to be messed with. We learned to say "Good Night" in greeting after a certain time in the evening rather than as a parting gesture. And after a while it all became normal.

One could easily recognize newcomers to the island when they were hitchhiking by the thumb they stuck out. Everyone who'd been on St. John for even a few weeks got used to pointing in the direction they were going with their index finger instead. We gave hardly a thought to seeing a person dressed in clothing finely stitched from burlap adorned with cloth remnants that gave it style and got used to seeing elderly ladies on Sunday morning walking long distances under the hot sun in beautiful snow-white dresses. These ladies always greeted us with a smile, but rarely accepted offers of a ride. And having someone on a street corner offer me a hibiscus flower for my hair, for no reason other than my hair had no adornment, was something I came to accept with a graceful smile.

Island vehicles were often adorned with the personality of their owners by a quirky decoration attached to the grillwork or in front of the windshield. Some were easy to figure out, like the Pillsbury doughboy that topped the baker's car, or the tiny hammer belonging to a local carpenter. Others made you wonder, like the Barbie doll from hell or the toilet bowl carefully perched to catch the rain. My downstairs neighbor had a live cactus growing from her car, while one lively grandma managed a daily fresh floral bouquet on hers.

Bob and I decided we, too, needed to make a statement. My husband chose his ornament rather quickly. A plastic Smurf cartoon character in a kayak, which he just happened to have, was his first choice. I had no sense of personal identity. An airplane would represent the travel I took regularly, but that was definitely an anti-island kind of thing. I didn't want a small computer, since it hardly represented my personality. My Brown Bay trail name was Ketch an' Keep Karin but only a few would recognize this local thorny plant hoisted on my vehicle. Besides, I wasn't sure that was a reputation I wanted to advertise. I finally settled on a goat skull I found one day that had no meaning and confused everyone. It wasn't me but still it was perfect.

Our friend Marvin who had a little sailboat on the front of his car told us he'd gotten a ticket for failing to yield at a newly erected but poorly positioned stop sign one day. We waited to hear the St. John twist his little story was sure to have. Our friend had told the officer he thought the stop sign had been put in the wrong place. Logic made it seem that the sign should have been placed on the intersecting side road, he explained, but agreed he'd broken the law and graciously accepted the ticket. The next morning Marvin received a phone call from the police. He was told to tear up the ticket he'd received the day before. The policeman had checked and sure enough, the sign had been placed in the wrong spot.

It was often difficult for the police and other public officials to deal with the peculiarities on St. John. Often policemen had been assigned to the island from St. Thomas and had no understanding of local landmarks. The intersection up on Gift Hill on St. John that for years everyone knew as the fork in the road was one such example. When a grass roots crime prevention group started in the area, the police insisted that official road signs were needed at all intersections for them to provide fast and accurate response. And so, a sign went up on the opposite side of the intersection from the plywood fork. Curious, one day I slowed down my Geo tracker in passing, to read the small black lettered words on the new white road sign. It read "FORK IN THE RD."... of course.

Chapter Fifteen
The Quiet Season

We looked forward to the seasonal downswing in visiting tourists and longed for the empty beaches we enjoyed the previous summer. Bob longed for less traffic on his regular trips to St. Thomas. But before it could happen, he would have to survive Carnival time on that island and months before St. John would host its own Carnival. When St. Thomas Carnival time arrived, Bob encountered parking lots turned into Carnival venues, new for parking cars along the waterfront, and increased traffic throughout. Companies he visited were working with skeleton staffs, as many employees took vacation or sick leave to take part in various events during the month long party. There was no way I could convince Bob to return for an evening or on the weekends to enjoy the festivities ourselves.

I resigned myself to reading about the venues in the daily papers and watching the various parades on TV. On the last day of the festivities, I had to travel through St. Thomas to the airport for a business trip to the states and left an hour early fearing big crowds in town. But downtown St. Thomas was deserted. All were sleeping off a long night the evening before and preparing for a longer finale later that day and night. I'd missed the St. Thomas Carnival completely my first year and I promised myself we'd take part when St. John's own Carnival time came this time around.

The fireworks on that last night were spectacular, I was told. Even Bob couldn't resist watching this Carnival climax. He even invited neighbors to our apartment for the event, since our balcony had the best view in the neighborhood. I got to see pictures of it in the paper when I returned home from my trip, but by then no one wanted to talk about Carnival time anymore.

Bob and I celebrated his twelfth month on-island by doing what we'd learned to do well. Packing and unpacking. This time I didn't argue. May is hurricane preparedness month in the USVI and Bob was determined to prepare early this year. We reviewed our pantry staples and made lists of things to stock up on just in case a disaster should strike. Batteries were checked and candles organized. Camping gear was sorted for things we might need easily available. We bought cases of drinking water and lots of bleach and other cleaning supplies. Then of course there was food to buy for our cats and for us too.

Past camping trips gave us experience in preparing appetizing meals from simple basics, which helped. We tried to think of everything like the need for comfort foods and foods with differing textures. If a hurricane struck, we were ready with pancake mix needing just the addition of water and our stock of maple syrup. Crunchy things like potato sticks and crackers were a necessity to break up any potential boredom from typical canned foods. Our pantry soon overflowed with staples enough to feed our whole neighborhood for weeks.

As the tourist season dwindled down, I started taking pottery-throwing lessons on St. Thomas. Commuting to and from class was a challenge. The VITRAN buses at the Red Hook dock were very sporadic and the open-aired gypsy taxis even less dependable. The air-conditioned taxi vans that pick up and drop off tourists at Red Hook was an expensive option and there were even fewer options for returning to the dock afterwards. Luckily, I was able to find someone at the pottery studio to drive me through the dark to Red Hook after class where I'd wait for forty-five minutes before catching the next ferry to St. John. After a time, I began to enjoy and look forward to that waiting time.

Arriving that early, only the taxi drivers were around. Most played dominos or cards to pass the time away. I always gave a "Good Night" greeting and sat on the edge of the dock to watch the fish feeding in the glow of the bright lights overhead. The fish were attracted to the lights and gave me quite a show. Sometime I'd see stingrays or flying fish fleeing from their prey. It was mesmerizing. Then the tourists began to appear in small groups and interrupted my solace with hesitant questions once they sized me up. With my clay stained casual clothing it only took them seconds to determine my St. Johnian status. The tourists always wanted to know where to eat, where to swim and where to shop and I enjoyed trying to be objective in figuring out what would please them.

The men working the dock sometimes taught me local slang and it's here that I learned the three-part and five-part handshakes that were unique to our area. Most locals arrived at the dock near the last minute, with their timing down pat. I'd come to know quite a few regulars and every week I met a few more. It was St. John Trivia time, taking the place of our Friday evenings out in Cruz Bay that had dwindled with the end of tourist season. On the docks of Red Hook, I found "belongin'".

On the weekends Bob and I saw fewer and fewer people on the beaches, but more and more that I personally knew by name. The seas were mostly calm and Bob and I spent lots of time floating our weekends away. Despite our hurricane preparedness, rain was hard to come by and we wavered between being glad and hoping for filled cisterns. When it seemed that a long lazy summer was finally upon us, St. John Carnival arrived to give us a jolt.

 A taxi driver on St. Thomas described the annual scene with acute accuracy. "You know how I know its Carnival on St. John? When I see Cruz Bay in the distance dip down into the water from the weight of the people. That's when I know for sure it's Carnival time."

He wasn't far off the mark. On tiny St. John, Carnival time brought huge crowds of people. For weeks before, there were signs of preparation as locals prepared their Carnival booths, repaired the roads, and added a touch of new paint to their buildings. Our Carnival this year coincided with the one hundred and fiftieth-year celebration of the Emancipation in the Virgin Islands and Carnival on St. John was expected to be larger than normal.

For weeks there were special Carnival and Emancipation celebration events to disrupt our tranquility. Calypso and Carnival Queen contests, Band jams and food fairs were the traditional crowd pleasers. Carnival Village, with its food and alcohol booths took over the parking lot across from the Post Office. The Bandstand in Cruz Bay's park was often the site of dance and musical events, along with every other bare and level space near Cruz Bay. Every night the Village was alive until the wee hours of the morning. The ferries extended their hours of operation and larger ticket booths were put up in Red Hook to handle the influx of visitors.

Bob and I managed a couple of rare nights out during the workweek to dance to the beats in Carnival village and try some devastating local alcoholic concoctions and to buy local crafts from artisans in the park. Tourists on their first visit to the island found it hard to believe St. John was known as the quiet island. During Carnival it became a wild and crazy place. I was determined to join in J'Ouvert, a traditional early morning march to the beat of load music through the streets of downtown Cruz Bay which started around four o'clock in the morning. My friends copped out, though, so I blissfully slept through the event. Moe and Bev, living in downtown, were not so lucky. They were woken at five o'clock in the morning with a start, thinking a riot had broken out. It was simply J'Ouvert, marching through their neighborhood. On July fourth, Carnival time came to its climax.

Bob was hoping to go to the beach, since everyone within five hundred miles would be in Cruz Bay to watch the parade. He didn't have a prayer, even when a morning rainstorm threatened the day. Peer pressure from the neighborhood convinced him to be a good sport and line the sidewalks with the rest of us. While the parade was scheduled for late morning, our arrival in early afternoon gave us plenty of time to select prime viewing space. My neighbor Jay and I managed to take some time and visit the crafters in the park and play tourist for a while. We bought matching straw hats and admired the newly erected Emancipation statue unveiled that day. The statue, its mirror images proudly erected on St. Croix and St. Thomas that same week, was placed at the front entrance to Cruz Bay Park to welcome all visitors to St. John. It's the bust of a former slave, with a conch horn held to his mouth to blare the news of emancipation and with a raised scythe in his other hand. The statue was reminiscent of the logo for all Emancipation celebration events throughout the Territory that year. Jay and I even posed with the statues to have our pictures taken with our new straw hats on our heads.

By mid-afternoon the streets were lined with crowds of people and the parade finally began. Every inch of free space held spectators, including any nearby roofs or tree. Our neighborhood was ready, content from our varied lunches culled from the various food booths everywhere downtown, and comfortable in our lawn chairs and hastily rigged umbrellas to shad the sun. We saw Mocko Jumbie troupes and the myriad of princes and princesses propped and waving from their sponsor's vehicles. The trailer beds with live bands made the ground shake below our feet. The handcrafted floats were interspersed with every kind of marching group you could imagine and the costumes were wild.

The parade moved sporadically past, and each short break in the action gave Woody's, the bar/restaurant across the street, the chance to send over fresh drinks and snacks to us hot weary spectators. They were doing a phenominal business, reminiscent of any night during tourist season. A Post Office worker marched by, decked out in an outrageous costume with feathers and streamers. His broad smile made him more unrecognizable than his costume did. One troupe carried fruit baskets and burlap sacks balanced on their heads as they bounced to the beat of the music marching behind them. Hours after it started, the parade was over and we all headed home to get ready for the finale.

As part of St. John Rescue, Bob had to help out that night during the fireworks display. He was stationed on the waterfront near the fireworks barge in the harbor. All boats were warned to leave their moorings for safety's sake and most took heed. Though he hated crowds, Bob had ended up right in the thick of things. I found a more sedate place to view the event, at a small party in a beautiful house perched above Cruz Bay overlooking the harbor. When the fireworks started only a few minutes late, I was duly impressed. They were spectacular.

It was the finale that was confusing, since rather than expected huge climax, the fireworks seemed to just dwindle away. The whole party was poised for the last big burst, but it never came. Only the smoky remains filled the night air until it drifted away to the distant beat of music from the Carnival Village below. Bob later told us that some of the fireworks fell onto the deck of the barge. They went off in a horizontal direction while the rest of the finale had fallen into the water itself. In a way, it was a better ending. The fireworks end left us all wanting more and ready for an even bigger celebration next year.

After Carnival, St. John became a sleepy place. There were parking spaces to be had in Cruz Bay and it was possible again to find beaches without another soul on them. I marveled that most tourists thought our summers to be hot. They sweltered in hundred degree heat waves, while gentle trade winds kept our weather wonderful. Summer brought warmer waters and calmer seas, just perfect for weekend floating in Paradise. For the first time in our lives, summer didn't pass too quickly. Work on the Brown Bay Trail slowed down, as the sun made the day hot, even in the early morning hours. Besides, this summer there were other adventures to keep everyone entertained.

An archeological dig began at Cinnamon Bay, just a few feet away from the beach's edge. It was a ceremonial Taino Indian site and just a few inches below the surface bits and pieces of shells and pottery were found dating from the fifteenth century. Under the guidance of professionals, everyone on-island was encouraged to volunteer and participate in the dig. It was fun sorting the bits and pieces found by size and type and sifting sand through the screens was something that brought back childhood fantasies. My friend Jan and our 'goat-girl' friend Jessie were the most consistent participants we knew. When Jessie uncovered a shell pendant one day, she was on top of the world. And, when she was given a commemorative T-shirt for all her hard work by the site's chief archeologist, her feet hardly touched the ground as she pranced around the neighborhood to show it off.

That summer, many of the women on the island enjoyed a girl's night out when an island-wide fashion show was held at the world-class Caneel Bay Resort. It was an evening filled with fun and entertainment and gave everyone a chance to dress up to kill without husbands to worry about. Best of all, it was a fundraiser for the Safety Zone, an organization dedicated to providing a safe haven for domestic violence victims. The Friends of the VI National Park offered an unusually inexpensive snorkel tour of the British Virgin Islands, and Bob and I were first in line to enjoy snorkeling at the Baths on Virgin Gorda. We even found time one weekend to spend a day of shopping together on St. Thomas and have dinner at a Chinese restaurant near Havensight.

Much public roadwork and construction got done that summer. We all dreaded the momentous change that made the South Shore Road a one way lane out from town, adding a long two-minute permanent detour to any rush to catch a ferry from our south shore apartment. Even worse, everyone who wasn't in a rush stopped each morning at Ronnie's Bakery for a quick coffee and pastry on their way to work. Now, everyone had to drive out of their way and head back out of town on the one-way road to make the stop. It took months and some serious creativity on Ronnie's part for the bakery's business to recover. Die-hards like Bob were happy with the inconvenience, since parking was easier and the early morning construction crews didn't gobble his fantastic pastries up before he got there.

No one minded the temporary five-minute detour caused by the anticipated re-paving of the hill known as Jacobs Ladder. When it rained or a water truck dripped water making the road wet, many vehicles couldn't make it up to the top and I was tired of driving behind trucks that lost their payload halfway up the hill. Knowledgeable locals stopped at the bottom of the hill to wait in safety while watching trucks carrying large loads ahead of them attempt the climb. When they stalled, the trucks had no other option but to back slowly down the hill and try again anyway.

Occasionally, a taxi would stop on an angle at the crest of the hill to drop off passengers. They were oblivious to any unwary driver behind them or cresting the other side of the hill. Tourists occasionally would attempt to turn around halfway up the hill once their vehicle stalled. It often resulted in disaster as their vehicle tipped over halfway through their turn. The road was narrow and there were no sidewalks. Many of the unfortunates had no other option than to walk up or down the steep hill to get to their destinations, regardless of traffic. And halfway up the hill lived a variety of goats and chickens that liked to cross the street at whim. St. Johnian drivers needed no yield sign to slow to a near stop before attempting Jacobs Ladder in either direction.

Jacobs Ladder got re-paved to a smooth black top finish after a couple of month's anticipation. It even got roadside walkways added for most of the way up the hill. But it barely got widened enough to accommodate these changes. And worse, the road did not get re-graded at the same time, so the steepness of the grade remained and the danger of striking a person walking just over the crest of the hill was the same. At least the potholes were finally gone.

All summer long Bob, like many islanders, kept a close eye on our cable TV's Weather channel. Surprisingly, the few tropical waves and tropical depressions that formed bypassed us with little rain or wind. We occasionally dipped into our hurricane supplies for odd items to consume while we became more and more convinced that there'd be no hurricane this year. The little Hurricane Erica from last season was a dim memory of our overkill in last year's preparations.

Then one day, a tropical depression appeared off the coast of Africa. Its mass was large and it was quickly picking up strength. Although all our tropical waves and depressions started this same way, somehow everyone on St. John knew that this was the one storm that could impact us this year. Tropical Storm Georges gained strength, stayed its path and still days away from our island it became a full fledge hurricane. At the time I was in Massachusetts, but even I knew in my heart that Georges would be coming to St. John soon. With still a couple of days to go Georges had gained so much strength it was escalated to a category five hurricane. The news brought fear to everyone, since a hurricane of such magnitude is very rare and extremely destructive.

Everyone, including Bob and I remembered the wrath brought to St. John in 1995 when Hurricane Marilyn, a mere category two hurricane, passed through. The hurricane had brought tornadoes along with the wind and the rain, and the destruction remained evident to this day in some places. I arrived back home on a half-empty airplane energized with the need to prepare for Georges' destruction. But, the first thing I did was to tape our hurricane map for the region on a wall in the apartment. The map had been saved from a *VI Daily News* newspaper at the beginning of the season. Then I marked it up with the latest storm coordinates.

Bob and I moved our outdoor furniture into the swimming pool, which is standard pre-hurricane procedure. The wind chimes, birdfeeders and hammocks were brought inside and packed away. Our bookcases were shrouded in plastic and all our clutter was packed in plastic bags. We sent off a round of e-mail messages to family, friends, and my workplace, then packed the equipment away in two layers of protective plastic. The tops of all tables and counters were made bare and our kitchen cabinets reorganized to make space for our small appliances. We taped out kitchen cabinets shut and wrapped everything else we could in plastic. The living room furniture was all piled together against an inside wall away from the windows and doors and covered with a huge tarp. Our floor space was made as bare as possible in case we had any flooding. The master bedroom was next, with a similar treatment, and even all our clothes were encased in plastic except for those few things we kept out for immediate use.

Our efforts weren't limited to our own apartment. Bob and I helped neighbors and businesses wherever we could. The island that weekend was a beehive of activity. We squeezed in a short hour at a beach for a 'sea bath' knowing it would be a while before we could do so again. The empty beach spoke volumes and we cut our visit short. Long into the nights that weekend we prepared, and although Georges had slowed down and had been downgraded to a category two hurricane, it was still coming right at us. No matter how I viewed the changing map coordinates, we were in for quite a storm. The emergency supply containers we'd organized in the spring came in handy, since we didn't have to search for flashlights or candles or radios or foodstuffs.

Stores in town stayed open late, but we were already prepared without dealing with the crowds. On Sunday night, with the hurricane less than twelve hours away, everyone we knew was cooking up a big batch of stew or chili or other concoction large enough to eat for days. Exhausted, I was in no mood to cook. We turned off the propane flow to our stove for the duration. Invitations came from five different people for Bob and I to stay with them if we weren't comfortable at our own apartment. As part of his St. John Rescue routine, Bob got a hurricane curfew pass that would save him from being arrested if a state of emergency were called. He then went to the designated St. John shelters to check in and help out, but the shelters had yet to open. Most people just hunkered down at home. And finally sometime after midnight, so did we.

The main force of the hurricane hit us just before mid-day on Monday. We'd lost our telephone and power and assumed everyone had. The first big gusts toppled a tan-tan tree next to our building that we'd been trying to convince Moe to trim back. There was no question the hurricane had arrived. Bob and I retreated to our apartment's guestroom with its three concrete walls. We coaxed the cats in with us. The fourth side of the tiny room was mostly a sliding door made of safety glass, but it was in the most sheltered area of the property and we hoped for the best. While Bob and I were adding the final touches of comfort to our well-sheltered cubbyhole, Jay and Andre were having a party. Their building was much more protected than ours since two-thirds of their apartment was backed up against a hillside.

Soon, the front side of our apartment began getting barraged by constant strong winds. Outdoors, the wooden enclosure for our propane tank blew off and onto the ground. With our neighbor Karen helping, we brought the loose boards into our apartment before they were lost forever. What one person could normally do took three people because of the winds. Soon afterwards, some unknown thing outside flew against our kitchen window and broke it. Our door and all the windows were pulsating and water began seeping under the door.

In our protected guestroom, the sounds of the storm were distant. A couple of hours into the hurricane, our neighbor Andre came up the spiral staircase next to our cubbyhole. His apartment had no phone outage and he and Jay were concerned about our safety. The walk from his building to ours was relatively protected from the winds, but Bob and I both thought he was crazy to be out during the storm.

"Is this where the hurricane is?" Andre asked in a little boy voice as he took a little walk around our porch toward the front of our building

Two seconds later he got his answer as he rounded the last corner and a blast of wind and rain almost knocked him over. Just then one of our gutters flew by. Andre quickly retreated to the relative safety of the back porch.

"Want a little tour of reality, neighbor?" Bob chided as he led Andre into our living room.

"Gee, you guys are over-prepared," Andre said as he spying our tarp-covered furnishings against the inner wall. But then Bob showed him the long blades of grass that had somehow wrapped themselves around the inside of our front door and the growing puddle on our living room floor that a mass of beach towels were trying to keep at bay. I showed him the broken window in the kitchen and the inch of standing water in the downstairs bathroom. Andre was duly humbled and impressed. He helped Bob shore up the kitchen window with duct tape and more plastic, then suggested we visit the party down at his place. Bob and I declined. It was time to wring out the towels and add more to barrier the water flowing in both upstairs and down.

At its worst, water flowed halfway across our bedroom from the lone bathroom window upstairs, despite regular towel wringing and sponging. The downstairs fared little better, as each of our windows on the front side of our house leaked like sieves. At some point, we noted that the ceiling was creaking and shaking in the wind, as the storm attempted to rip it apart. The loud noise of the storm made it difficult to talk and we worked the towels quickly, anxious each time to finish and return to the relative safety of our guestroom. Our cats were smart enough to stay in the guestroom where it was relatively quiet and safe.

Our crazy neighbor Andre returned. This time he had a rope attached between him and his daughter Jessie, and he had strangers behind them.

"Everyone wants to see the hurricane," he said as he led the party around the side of our porch.

"You're crazy," I told them all. "The hurricane eye is just south of here right now."

A few seconds later they were all back, as the storm winds were too strong for anyone to do more than peek around the corner without being blown away. Those people with their curiosity were more likely to be harmed by the hurricane than we were and we urged them to go home and get a life. They just didn't grasp the danger that flying objects could cause.

The darkness that night was oppressive, and our candles and flashlights and radio were our only companions. Each time new storm coordinates were announced I took a flashlight into the hallway and marked them on our hurricane map. Our cats were happy to stay in the guestroom and cuddle next to Bob. The storm continued late into the night and somehow we both finally dropped off to a deep, exhausted sleep.

Chapter Sixteen

The Grass Is Greener . . .
After It Rains

The next morning, the stuffiness of our room woke us early. Quickly, Bob and I made our way outside. Our swimming pool was almost black from the soil and leaves and other debris that the storm had deposited and the pool furniture was invisible under the sludge. The rain was long gone and the passing clouds promised a beautiful day. Bob and I searched the hillsides around us, but could only see one home that had any apparent damage. We could see houses that had previously been hidden through the dense foliage. The palm and papaya trees and most other plants had been stripped bare of their leaves. It was hard to believe that less than twenty-four hours had passed.

Bob and I were not alone. Karen, Ricky, Jay, Andre, Jessie, Pam and our other neighbors had also emerged into the sunlight and were gingerly dodging fallen wires as they surveyed the damage. Some came together and embraced as though lifetime had just passed. Our two cats refused to venture more than ten feet beyond the building boundaries. We were all numb from the past twenty-four hours.

My car was tucked tightly between other vehicles in a protected area below our home. It was covered with debris, but intact and surprisingly dry despite the soft convertible top. Strong wind had blown minute debris into every seam and sealed them from the heavy rains. Bob's car was intact but unmovable due to my paranoia over just what types of utility lines were draped behind it.

Soon the occasional vehicle passed slowly by as drivers queried if all was okay. The owners of Bob's company even stopped by to see if we needed any help. Bestech, like most companies on the island, was closed. Chuck and his wife Diane were on their way to town to survey the damage. Without a telephone, I was cut off from work, but there was little time to ponder the problem.

Bob and I began the tedious task of ringing out the numerous towels on the floors and mopping up the standing water remaining. Eighteen towels were hung from our porch railing to dry along with damp clothes that covered every surface. The outside of our building was plastered with a thin layer of debris that quickly dried in the hot sun and defied all attempts short of a pressure washer to remove it. Karen convinced us the wires draped behind Bob's car were just phone and cable TV wires. She'd lived through multiple hurricanes on St. John and she was sure. This thrilled Bob, as he was anxious to be out on the road to check the islands' shelters and offer assistance if needed.

While Bob went off for his joy ride, I tested our propane tanks and began removing furniture from the black hole that was our swimming pool. All of Cruz Bay was under generator power, Bob told me when he returned, and Marina Market and the St. John Ice Company were already open for business. The local dry cleaners where Jay worked was also open and she was there with nary a customer in sight except Bob. My husband had had the unusual foresight to put a load of laundry in the car before he left for town.

The huge blocks of ice he brought home arrived just in time to save lots of foodstuffs that would otherwise required throwing out. Our various assortment of ice coolers were lined up as I worked frantically to sort refrigerator items based on how quickly they'd perish. Some blocks of ice had to be cracked into little chunks to fit the smallest ice coolers. It was worth it, as our full freezer was thawing like crazy and leaving puddles on the kitchen floor. By the time the transfers were completed, we had very wet muddy floors. Again we mopped and wrung out towels. By the time we were done, daylight was gone. A mandatory 8:00 PM curfew made the night eerily quiet and let us fall into an exhausted sleep quickly.

The next morning, Moe brought up a generator that the two buildings could share. It saved most of our foodstuffs. The generator gave us toilets again to everyone's great relief as we strove to return to normal. Surprisingly, our television worked off the generator, but without cable, we got only two English stations. The national news said the Virgin Islands had been devastated but friends and neighbors and even our own eyes assured us it wasn't true. Many telephones on St. John had remained working throughout the storm, but no one could call long distance. There was no way to reassure relatives or friends outside of the Virgin Islands for two long days.

A day after the hurricane passed, Bob was back at work and extremely busy. I managed to unpack my notebook computer and put in a few hours of work using my battery pack and extra power from our generator running through an uninterruptable power supply (UPS) device. It became quickly obvious I needed a telephone. Diane, her home high up on the hill overlooking Rendezvous Bay, had a satellite telephone and a satellite system for her television. When she heard the Virgin Islands were decimated on a national news network, she decided to take action on behalf of all of us. She dialed the network, demanded they retract their story and accurately report on the facts. Her efforts made her a heroine to everyone I knew.

As soon as long distance service was restored, I put my work contingency plans into action. Chuck had kindly offered me the use of an empty classroom to work from at his Bestech offices in town. I spent hours making phone calls and catching up on my e-mail, but the small windowless, air-conditioned room made me claustrophobic. The next day, I set up shop at Jay's house once everyone there was gone to work or school for the day. It was only a two-minute walk from all of my file folders and other work paraphernalia. Thanks to the kindness of these kind folks, I was able to function for the six long workdays before my own telephone was finally restored.

Without ceiling fans constantly moving the air along, our apartment stayed rather stuffy, despite leaving the doors and windows open whenever we could. The small generator needed to rest at night, so even a small floor fan was out of the question. Bob and I were concerned about mosquitoes and other flying creatures of the night, but solved that problem by finally hoisting the mosquito net I'd gotten years ago over our bed. Swimming in the pool wasn't an option to cool down and even the beaches were declared off limits until lab tests were done to check the water quality.

Then came the mutant mosquitoes. Instead of the occasional bug, we'd become inundated with these flying bloodsuckers. No one on the island was immune. These large parasites seemed to enjoy the taste of most mosquito sprays. We used five cans in less than five days, and still we had bites all over ourselves. Only when Bob and I were tucked under our mosquito net at night were we protected.

It took only one night for the cats to figure out how to slide in between the mosquito net and the mattress. They too preferred sleeping away from the flying creatures every night. It was a great relief when we got power back five days after Georges passed by. But by then, we liked the idea of the mosquito net and the added protection it gave us when we sporadically lost power at night as we did almost every week. The mosquito net became a normal part of our sleeping environment from that point forward.

Eight days after Hurricane Georges, our telephone lines were back up and working. I was in heaven. Our swimming pool was beginning to get back to normal, but I wasn't ready to risk a swim. The amount of chlorine used to shock the pool back to normal would probably have bleached my body white. Finally, the beaches were declared safe. Two weeks after Georges, Bob and I spent a whole day at the beach floating and ignoring reality.

It would take another month before our TV's cable access was back, but we didn't have to miss most prime time shows. Diane taped shows religiously on her satellite TV to pass onto us less fortunate souls. And the CNN Network came to our rescue when they allowed our Public Broadcasting System to air a half-hour of national and world news four times a day. Our own TV got mostly Spanish stations without our cable hook-up and after a few weeks Bob and I decided to take Spanish lessons.

Some of St. Johnians missed Hurricane Georges and its immediate aftermath by being off island for business or vacation when the storm hit. Our friend Jan was one of these. Unaware of the pending storm, she had gone to Chicago for long needed vacation only days before the hurricane hit. Jan was facing a crossroad in her life and trying to decide whether to make a long-term commitment to St. John or move on in search of some other Paradise. She hoped a little time off island would help her decide what to do.

Right before we lost our telephone line in the hurricane, Jan called with offers to bring back any anticipated emergency supplies that we hadn't had time to buy ourselves. Bob took advantage of the situation by requesting a portable twelve-volt boat fan, for whatever purpose I could only guess. He said he could rig it to run off a battery that he could recharge during the day from a generator. I thought he was nuts. So much for my rugged adventurer who needed no modern conveniences - Bob was clearly a spoiled material kind of guy.

When Jan returned ten days after hurricane Georges, she had Bob's fan in tow. Our power was back on, but Bob was still happy to see a new toy.

Our friend also had the foresight to bring a caseload of mosquito spray, enough for the entire neighborhood. The mutants were in full force by then and we were all grateful. I told Jan she was lucky to miss all the excitement, but was surprised when she shook her head.

"I know my worries and concerns were like nothing you all went through, but it was just awful. The news said the islands had been devastated and I couldn't get through on the telephone. For days I tried to get news and I worried about everyone and everything. Friends and family up north said at least I was home when the disaster struck, but that's when it hit me. Chicago isn't my home. St. John is my home now."

We'd known Jan belonged on St. John and it was wonderful she'd finally figured it out herself. While I'd been anxious for friends in New England to know we were okay after the hurricane, I was more concerned about the people who'd become my own extended local family. Neither Bob nor I had any thoughts of leaving to avoid the cleanup or the mosquitoes or the aggravations of getting our lives back to normal. This was our home now too.

In the wake of Hurricane Georges, lots of iguanas lost their secluded nests, but survived. On the short stretch of road to Cruz Bay I saw no less than six separate huge iguanas traversing the roads one morning. The papaya tree in front of our house grew back its beautiful foliage fast and many trees and bushes on the island were soon fooled into blossoming off-season flowers. The hurricane had forced Bob and I to do an island version of spring-cleaning and got us all to reassess our priorities.

Some things may never be the same. The gutters that came off our upper roof proved to be a blessing in disguise. Before, most rainstorms caused rain to rush down the upper gutters so fast that water gushed off the lower roof and onto the ground. Now the rain flowed more evenly into the lower gutters and into our cistern. The plywood fork in the road symbol had lost a tine, but had survived. In fact, it was now a more accurate depiction of the real fork in the road it described. The shiny white 'FORK IN THE RD.' sign was intact, but it was now turned at an angle that was more accurate. My favorite tree on the island, a beautiful pomegranate, was doomed because of windburn.

No one in our Adopt A Trail group seemed anxious to visit the Brown Bay Trail after Georges. Everyone told me that nature had probably undone all the hard work and effort that we'd put into it and no one had the energy to start all over again. Eventually, I went by myself without any tools just to survey the damage. I'd convinced myself that the hurricane had actually helped to widen the trail. The normally dry East End of St. John was dense with new foliage though, and by the time I reached the trailhead, my expectations were low.

The beginning of the trailhead had never been cleared more than the modest widening I'd insisted on to discourage the Ketch an Keep plants from attaching themselves to me with any step I took. Still, it was narrow enough to discourage tourists from wandering up the hill until the whole trail was up to par. I found the path now lined with a beautiful array of short bushy flowers of all colors of the rainbow. There was a strong woodsy smell in the air that reminded me of a deep dark decaying forest. As I started up the path, the woodsy scent gave way to a beautiful fragrance that became more exotic and rare with every step I took. Unknown flowering vines created a loose shaded canopy overhead. Our hard work had not been in vain.

I was able to make it up the first third of the trail to the top of the ridge with only five fallen trees in the way. To be honest, two of these were mere branches, but without tools or gloves, I made no attempt to move them. Still our path was clearly visible and thanks to all our hard work, not one ketch an' keep plant caught me in its grasp. In one short morning our Brown Bay crew could bring the front of the trail back up to snuff and the fragrant beauty surrounding them would make the work pleasant. If only I could convince them to try. On my way back to the car, I pondered the problem and decided to let island time lull them all back to this special place.

Two short months later, our lives were to change again. Moe and Bev were decided to exclusively lease the apartment buildings many of us lived in to the Westin resort as part of a plan to sell them the property. The Westin was desperate for apartments for their employees to live in. My friends and I were all to become homeless just at the start of tourist season. It was a disaster. For every advertisement in Connections there were at least twelve desperate people vying for the privilege of a new place to live. Apartments were so hard to find that Doug Franklin, owner of the only long-term rental agency on the island, changed his answering machine to warn off prospective clients.

The island grapevine was everyone's saving grace. Like a hurricane aftermath, everyone shared tips. Places that weren't on the market yet and even some apartments beneath private homes that were in process of being built yielded opportunities. Nothing was ever definite until deposits were paid and move dates were down to two weeks. So, everyone had secret back-up possibilities in case their first choice didn't work out.

Bob and I were pushed into making a life decision. We knew we'd be living on St. John for the foreseeable future and we had some cash reserves. So along with apartments, we looked at homes and condos on the lower end of the market. In the process, we explored nooks and crannies on St. John that boggled the mind. A two room shack on top of a mountain with a gorgeous view and a high-tech rental apartment with an electronic hurricane shutter for a front door were both considered options. We were pickier than most and the pickings were slim, but we were persistent.

In seemingly no time at all, Bob and I had put a deposit on a place of our own. We settled on one of the few condos available that allowed year-round owner occupancy. Most complexes were geared strictly for the short-term rental market and year-round residents weren't allowed. Cost of ownership was high everywhere, and we could only afford a one-bedroom condo. We weren't quite ready to own a house yet anyway and the small space meant less to keep clean. Yard sales and consolidating our possessions again would be necessary to fit into the smaller space. Still, Bob somehow managed to make another pipe dream come true. He would soon be a partial owner of a nice sized swimming pool that would daily beckon below our huge outside porch.

Last week, as we packed to move into the condo, a strong storm front passed by. Known locally as a 'tropical wave', it brought lots of rain. A couple of days later, the termites swarmed outside on our porch. This time we were ready for the onslaught. Our cats enjoyed the show from inside our darkened apartment while Bob turned porch lights on for their viewing enjoyment. In the dim glow of the outside bulbs, I planted tomato seeds in little pots with renewed hope for a year of bounty at our new home.

Yesterday morning, Bob got e-mail from a kayaker friend up north. With it came an offer to sell Bob's drysuit, which was still stored in New England, to another boater. My husband got excited about the prospect and immediately replied that he wanted to sell it. While Bob was unloading his past, some things from my past were coming back home, just in time for our move.

A neighbor had dropped off a copy of *The VI Daily News* at our place over breakfast, and while Bob played with the computer, I perused the news. Included in this edition was the newspapers' regular 'Police Reports' column with police logs from St. John. The first entry I read was a complaint from a man who'd seen someone wearing a pair of his boots in Cruz Bay. Those boots had purportedly been stolen from the man some time ago. A few entries further down in the newspaper column was one that noted a pair of boots had been returned to their rightful owner. As I chuckled over this tidbit, someone knocked on our door . . .

"Are any of these yours?" asked a brawny man with his head buried behind a mountain of shoes. Was this man the 'boot burglar' trying to make restitution for his crimes? Stunned by the thought, I was caught between gaping and laughing at the crazy sight before me.

"Or, do you know who any of these belong to?" the man added despairingly.

A while back, I'd lost a pair of sneakers and some sandals when I'd left them outside our front door while cleaning. Sure enough, as the man twirled slowly in a half-circle, I spied my very own sneakers dangling by their ties from the man's right elbow. My discovery brought a frown to my face.

"Which ones are yours?" the relieved man asked, with sagging shoulders. "I'm not a thief," he added, as a way to begin explaining the whole story.

It seems that the man's one year old dog had developed a shoe fetish, but had kept it hidden from his owner for quite some time. Judging from the quantity and variety of shoes the man carried, this dog has a real problem. The owner had discovered the huge cache of shoes by accident a couple of hours earlier. He was trying in vain to make everything right, but everyone he met thought he was the infamous 'boot burglar'. Watching him continue down the road two sneakers and three sandals lighter, I could only hope that he'd find the other owners soon.

Across the road and looking east, I can just see the vacation villa we rented with family/friends a couple of years ago. I remember how we'd all shared expenses to afford the luxurious three-bedroom villa with its courtyard pool on a small private peninsula for that last vacation to Paradise. Every day we'd played and the word 'work' was not in our vocabulary. Every night we ate in fine restaurants and daily we spent some time on our private beach. The villa itself was fantasy retreat - the word 'perfect' comes to mind. Bob and I are unlikely to experience such splendor again on St John, even for a week, but it doesn't matter. Now when I see the landmark roof of that vacation villa less than a mile away, there's no longing in my heart. Instead, I feel a soaring of the spirit and smile at the possibilities and the adventures life has to offer.

With a silly grin, I find myself saying "Good Afternoon" to the feral donkey grazing across the street. This tail swishing island neighbor is a reminder that Bob and I have come a long way in the past year. A year ago today it was just another normal day in Paradise and my naivete was evident. The scent of jasmine kissed the air, while hummingbirds fluttered nearby. St. Thomas formed a distant backdrop to this island panorama. Our covered porch was a perfect workplace for me, with mild trade winds mellowing the sun and wind chimes providing subtle background music. Down a short staircase, our inviting little swimming pool warmed in the garden splendor.

I had some paperwork to do, and could think of no better place to work. By break time, the pool would be ready to soothe. Moving my home office outdoors for the morning was a brilliant idea. My creative energy was strong and my work focus was singular. In a short time, I was completely engrossed in my work. And so the morning progressed until an unpleasant smell wafted through my Paradise. Its presence was distracting. At first I thought it just a quirk of the breeze carrying the memory of a garbage truck going down the hill. It happens occasionally, even in Paradise. The smell got stronger. My paperwork was lost to annoyance. I caught a movement out of the corner of my eye. Assuming a neighbor was heading for the pool, I turned to comment, with a complaint on my lips.

There are neighbors and there are 'neighbors'. These neighbors were three wild donkeys who'd come to visit. What a visit! They were just yards away drinking from our garden-side pool. As I watched, horrified, they proceeded to feed on all my downstairs neighbor Ricky's favorite potted plants. With a single bite, whole branches were defoliated. The foul stench ebbed and flowed with every movement they made. I shouted and I screamed, my work long forgotten, but no amount of noise seemed to bother these hungry beasts. Where were the neighborhood dogs when you needed them? Disgusted, I gave up. The donkeys had won. By the time I'd reorganized my paperwork and retreated inside, the donkeys were gone, and the garden devastation complete. Their stench remained for hours.

Of course, since I got smarter and received a 175-XXX double-barreled squirt gun for Christmas that can shoot water over fifty feet away, the donkeys don't seem to come around any more. Like this morning's visitor across the road, they seem to keep their distance. Perhaps they heard about Karin and Bob's donkey defense system through the island grapevine. If the donkeys ever do show up again at our new home, I'm well prepared. And in a devilish way, I'm looking forward to it.

Walking past my car with the goat skull on its front grate, I wonder what the next year will bring? Surely, Bob and I will learn to be more in harmony with the seasons of St. John. We now have close friends scattered throughout the island to visit and share adventures with. Maybe we'll finish bringing the Brown Bay Trail up to VINP specs and hike it for pure enjoyment without any tools in hand. Or maybe we'll find some other place to make special. To date we've only driven a small portion of the back roads on St. John and there are many ruins and hiking trails still to explore. Bob and I have only been to thirty of the supposed thirty-nine beaches on this island Paradise and there are still dozens of Cays nearby that we haven't kayaked past.

Maybe our old neighborhood group will get it together and have our own float in next year's St. John Carnival parade. We've been toying with the idea of a float dedicated to the snowbirds that visit each year, with a fake ski slope and a live snowman. There would be lots of soap-flake snow and Styrofoam snowballs we could throw at the crowd. Of course, this would all require planning and commitment and effort - maybe we'll just talk about it and convince someone else to do all the hard work as a fundraiser for some good cause. Then we can all get together on the sidelines, sit back under our umbrellas, enjoy the Carnival parade and cheer them on.

This afternoon, the sun is shining bright and the trade winds are steady. Still, from my viewpoint overlooking Rendezvous Bay, the water looks smooth as glass. Bob and I are putting aside our weekend chores this afternoon and sneaking away to a little cove we know for some fun. The snow-floats are already loaded into the car. With the warm sun washing away our worries and the quiet waters slowly drifting us along, we'll smile as tourists take our pictures from far away overlooks. If we get really energetic, Bob and I might even turn towards each other and, as we do so often, spontaneously whisper in unison "We LIVE here, now!"

Ah, Paradise!

A Special Note from the Author

The taxi drivers, shopkeepers, street vendors, government workers, National Park Service employees and in fact - all residents of the USVI - work hard to make sure our islands are a memorable Paradise for all our visitors.

Their caring and consistent desire to make visitors welcome is a big part of what makes this a Paradise. Pristine beaches and perfect weather are only the beginning.

I thank them for their continued efforts, and count myself blessed to be part of this fine community!

Island Car

(Written and recorded by Michael Beason, {aka: 'the ice cream dealer'}, and presented here by his kind permission)

Saw an ad in the paper, it said "Island Car,
Only eight hundred dollars, run good so far"
So I went to see what kind of car they had,
And for eight hundred dollars it was not too bad
It was once a jeep but it's now half wood,
And the brakes are broken but the horn works good
the lights all work unless it rains,
and the windshield wipers do the same.

(chorus)
It's an island car, it's an island car
In the USA it wouldn't be get you far
But in sweet St. John its only nine miles long
It's an island car, you can't go wrong

The bottom's rusted out and the spare tire's missin'
When it overheats you hear it hissin'
The seats fall over but the seat belts work,
And the clutch is so bad it'll never jerk
You can't fall in love nor even in lust
Because before to long it'll just be rust
An island car really sets you free
Cause in your heart you know it's temporary.

(chorus)
It's an island car, it's an island car
In the USA it wouldn't be get you far
But nothing here's far from anywhere
It's an island car, you can't go wrong

It's got no fourth gear, you don't need it here
And the sticker's good 'til sometime next year
Uphill it's slow, but there's the radio
Downhill you can pass if they go too slow
It's painted purple so it looks real sharp
I made myself a top with a FEMA tarp
The hood is loose and it's got no trunk
And it can drive itself if you get too drunk.

(chorus)
It's an island car, it's an island car.
In the USA, It wouldn't get you far,
But the motor runs, and the wheels ain't square
It's an island car, it'll get you there

Afterword

The FORK IN THE RD." remains a St. Johnian landmark, but the piece of plywood that gave the road it's name is history. It was replaced by an exact replica of the original plywood fork, but this one is made of concrete. Steve, the sign's architect and a resident of the FORK IN THE RD., even painted this new fork the same gaudy green as the plywood one. Many residents didn't notice the fork had turned to concrete at first.

When a vehicle, backed up one day and demolished the concrete fork, though, the island grapevine was quick to notice. Only days later, a two foot-high black iron fork was propped in its place. The fork continues its reincarnations to this day . . . check it out!

And thank you, Steve, for making sure that this island icon endures for a long time to come.

Desiring Paradise
Order Form

If you'd like more copies of this book:

❏   send _____ copies of *Desiring Paradise*

❏   send information about upcoming books

Name: _____

Address: _____

City: _____

State: _____ Zip Code: _____

Phone Number: _____ e-mail: _____

Payment Method: ❏   Personal Check   ❏   Money Order

Price: $19.95

Shipping: $4.00 for first copy and $2.00 for every copy thereafter.

Send payment and completed order form to:

Conch Publications

PO Box 1599

St. John, USVI   00831-1559

or e-mail us at kaybob@islands.vi - We'd love to hear from you!